THE BALKAN EXPRESS

FRAGMENTS FROM THE OTHER SIDE OF WAR

Slavenka Drakulić

THE BALKAN EXPRESS

FRAGMENTS FROM THE OTHER SIDE OF WAR

HarperPerennial
A Division of HarperCollins*Publishers*

A Dinner at the Harvard Club, Paris — Vukovar, It's Hard to Kill a Man, My Mother Sits in the Kitchen Smoking Nervously, An Actress Who Lost Her Homeland, If I Had a Son, What Ivan Said translated from the Croatian by Maja Soljan

This book was originally published in the United States in 1993 by W. W. Norton & Company. It is here reprinted by arrangement with W. W. Norton & Company.

HarperCollins books may be purchased for educational, business, or sales promotional use. For information please write: Special Markets Department, HarperCollins Publishers, Inc., 10 East 53rd Street, New York, NY 10022.

First HarperPerennial edition published 1994.

Library of Congress Cataloging-in-Publication Data

Drakulić, Slavenka, 1949–
      The Balkan express : fragments from the other side of war / Slavenka Drakulić. — 1st Harper Perennial ed.
      p.   cm.
      Originally published: New York : W.W. Norton & Co., 1993.
      ISBN 0-06-097608-X (pbk.)
      1. Yugoslav War, 1991– . 2. Drakulić, Slavenka, 1949– . I. Title.
[DR1313.D73   1994]
949.702′4—dc20   94-4862

94 95 96 97 98 RRD 10 9 8 7 6 5 4 3 2 1

CONTENTS

CONTENTS

TO MY DAUGHTER RUJANA

He worked by the barbed wire and heard awful screams.
His field was there?
Yes, right up close. It wasn't forbidden to work there.
So he worked, he farmed there?
Yes. Where the camp is now was partly his field. It was off limits, but they heard everything.
It didn't bother him to work so near those screams?
At first it was unbearable. Then you got used to it.

Dialogue with a villager from present-day Treblinka about living close to the concentration camp at the time of extermination of the Jews (from *Shoah – the Complete Text of the Film by Claude Lanzmann*, Pantheon Books)

Introduction

THE OTHER SIDE OF WAR

Barely a year and a half ago I was sitting in my apartment in Zagreb, looking at CNN reports from Baghdad and thinking, 'God, how could those people live there?' For many years I'd wondered the same about Beirut. Now I am sitting in the same place watching CNN reports on Sarajevo or Slavonski Brod, but I don't ask myself that question any more. After a year of war in Croatia and Bosnia and Herzegovina, after the destruction of entire cities like Vukovar, after the shelling of Osijek and Dubrovnik, foreign friends ask me, 'How is it possible to live in a country at war, how do you live there?' But now I understand that the answer is not simple and it doesn't come easily.

Here in Zagreb we haven't suffered severe casualties. Indeed, if you were to come here today you'd think that there was no war on. But that would be an illusion. The war is also here, it just affects us in a different way. At first there is a feeling of bewilderment. The war is like a monster, a mythical creature coming from somewhere far away. Somehow you refuse to believe that the creature has anything to do with your life, you try to convince yourself that everything will remain as

1

it was, that your life will not be affected, even as you feel it closing in around you. Finally the monster grabs you by the throat. You breathe in death, it impregnates your sleep with nightmare visions of dismembered bodies, you begin to picture your own end.

As the war goes on you create a parallel reality: on one side you neurotically cling to what used to be your everyday routine, pretending normality, ignoring the war. On the other side you are unable to deny the deep changes in your life and yourself, the shift in your values, emotions, reactions and behaviour. (Can I buy shoes, does it make any sense? Am I allowed to fall in love?) In war, the way you think of your life and what is essential to it totally changes. The simplest things no longer have the same weight or meaning. That is when you really know the war is on, that it has got to you too.

I used to think that war finally reached you through fear, the terror that seizes your whole being: wild heartbeats exploding, a wave of cold sweat, when there is no longer any division between mind and body, and no help. But war is more perverse.

It doesn't stop with the realization of your victimization, it goes deeper than that. War pushes you to the painful point where you are forced to realize and acknowledge the way you participate in it, become its accomplice. It may be a seemingly ordinary situation that makes you aware that you have become a collaborator – a thoughtless remark about why a refugee friend still needs high-heeled shoes, whatever.

War also heightens your awareness of the outside world. Astonishment gives way to anger, then resignation at the way Europe perceives this war – 'ethnic conflict', 'ancient legacy of hatred and blood-shed'. In this way the West tells us, 'You are not Europeans, not even Eastern Europeans. You are Balkans, mythological, wild, dangerous Balkans. Kill yourselves, if that is your pleasure. We don't understand what is going on there, nor do we have clear political interests to protect.'

The myth of Europe, of our belonging to the European family and culture, even as poor relations, is gone. We have been left alone with our newly-won independence, our new states, new symbols, new autocratic leaders, but with no democracy at all. We are left standing on a soil slippery with blood, engulfed in a war that will go on for God knows how long.

After a year of violence, with the dead numbering approximately 200,000, with many more wounded and over two million refugees flooding Europe, there came the story of the concentration camps. And all of a sudden in a thin desperate man behind barbed wire the world recognized not a Moslem, but a human being. That picture, the words 'concentration camp' and 'holocaust' finally translated the true meaning of 'ethnic cleansing'. At last people in the West began to grasp what was going on. It was suddenly clear that Europe hadn't learnt its lesson, that history always repeats itself and that someone is always a Jew. Once the concept of 'otherness' takes root, the unimaginable becomes possible. Not in some mythological country but to ordinary urban citizens, as I discovered all too painfully.

Finally, a few of words about this book. This is not the book about the war as we see it every day on our television screens or read about it in the newspapers. *Balkan Express* picks up where the news stops, it fits somewhere in between hard facts and analysis and personal stories, because the war is happening not only at the front, but everywhere and to us all. I am speaking about the other, less visible side of war, the way it changes us slowly from within. If my short half-stories, half-essays are to convey anything to the reader, it is this: the change in values, in one's way of thinking, one's perception of the world, that occurs on the inner side of war – a change that overtakes the inner self until one can scarcely recognize oneself any longer.

Unable as I was to separate myself from this war, the reader will undoubtedly notice inconsistencies in my own views, opinions and emotions. I don't apologize for that, because this is precisely what I wanted to write about. I offer only one piece of background information: the stories were written between April 1991 and May 1992, and are presented in more or less chronological order. They started as a few irregular contributions to various magazines and newspapers (*The Nation*, *New Statesman and Society*, *Die Zeit*, *Time*), but as the war came closer the urge to write about it and nothing else grew stronger and stronger. I ended up writing a book because, in spite of everything, I still believe in the power of words, in the necessity of communication. This is the only thing I know I believe in now.

ZAGREB
JUNE 1992

1

DINNER AT THE HARVARD CLUB

I'm going home, I think as the plane takes off above the Atlantic and, hovering for a brief moment above the slanted picture of Manhattan, dives upwards into the fluffy milky-white clouds. The sky above the clouds is crystal blue and so calm it seems almost indifferent. It would be wonderful to stay up there and coast awhile in the cool expanse of the azure void. I have just lost my link with land, the land beneath me and my own land to which I am about to return.

Only ten days have passed since I left. In these ten days another twelve people have been killed. The accumulating deaths make the wall dividing us from Europe and the world even higher and more formidable, placing us not only on the other side of the border but on the other side of reason too. This is why going back to my country – is it still called Yugoslavia? – this time feels different, more difficult than ever before: the word 'home' sticks in my throat, as if I would choke on it if I tried to say it out loud. I know that I'm going to be plunged deep into a black soupy tar, turgid and clammy, into the everyday which nobody understands any more. Already it is tugging at me from afar with long, thin tentacles.

Only last night I was having dinner in the elegant club of Harvard University in Cambridge, Massachusetts, in a Victorian building with mahogany-panelled drawing-rooms adorned with crystal chandeliers, thick burgundy-red carpets and mouldings on the ceilings. In this other reality where everything is logical, familiar and open to explanation, life runs smoothly as if governed by a huge, invisible, precise mechanism. After the first course – salad with walnuts and Roquefort dressing – my friends, considerate as they are, asked with concern about the situation. What is really going on? Will Yugoslavia fall apart? Will there be a civil war? 'You know,' my American friend, fiftyish, well-educated and well-informed, said apologetically, 'our press doesn't cover the events in your country regularly and when, after a month or two, a new article on Yugoslavia is published, the reader has already lost the thread.' I remembered the article in that morning's *New York Times* with a title perplexing in its ignorance: *Two Yugoslav factions blame each other for deaths in the conflict*. It was another in a whole series of articles which keep on repeating that Zagreb is the capital of Croatia, and Serbia and Croatia are the two largest of the six republics. And of course they published another map of Yugoslavia, not much bigger than a postage stamp, on which the rebel region around Knin appeared to cover nearly half of Croatia.

Silent-footed waiters brought salmon steaks in sauce Provençale with fried onions. We were eating, but somehow absent-mindedly. For a while my friends' questions seemed to bob in the air above the dinner plates and the tender, pinkish meat. There was nothing else for me to do but reach for a piece of paper from my purse and draw a map, somewhat different from the one in the *New York Times*, but a map nevertheless,

6

with republics and provinces, with Zagreb and Belgrade, with the Adriatic Sea, Knin and Borovo Selo. I really wanted them to understand this immensely complicated political situation. They wanted to understand, too. We bent our heads over the piece of paper with the roughly sketched contours of a country which was about to disappear; it was vanishing right in front of our very eyes, sensing that its tragedy could no longer be contained in words. I talked until my voice grew faint – the salmon steaks were getting cold and a thin skin was forming on the sauce – while my friends tried to trace the intricate line of causes and consequences, consequences and causes, as if that still mattered or as if knowing could change anything.

The situation seems symbolic: in a rich people's club, with soft background glissandos on the harp being played by a fragile-looking lady of uncertain age, over coconut ice-cream decorated with raspberries and weak, decaffeinated coffee, my hosts nod their heads over the Balkan tragedy. Of course they understand what it is all about, but their understanding – as well as everybody else's – reaches only a certain point. So far as some logic of events can be discerned and explained so good; we are still within the realm of reason. But finally there must and does come the question why, which is the hardest to answer because there are hundreds of answers to it, none of them good enough. No graphics, drawings or maps can be of any genuine help, because the burden of the past – symbols, fears, national heroes, mythologies, folksongs, gestures and looks, everything that makes up the irrational and, buried deep in our subconscious, threatens to erupt any day now – simply cannot be explained. I see the interest and concern on the faces of my friends being replaced by weariness and then resignation.

At that moment I can easily imagine the face of a Bush or a

Mitterrand, a Kohl or a Major, at first eagerly paying attention to the report given by an expert consultant who comes from this part of the world over the plate of clear bouillon and then perhaps some light plain-cooked white fish, only to shake his head wearily at the end of the dinner, lifting a silver spoon of slightly quivering crême caramel, admitting that he cannot understand, not fully, that madness, the Balkan nightmare. The consultant – a man tied to the war-plagued country by duty or by birth – feels that he is faced with a lack of understanding not only across the table but somehow across time. And while Mitterrand thoughtfully sips his Cointreau and then gently wipes the beads of perspiration on his upper lip with a napkin, the consultant or minister realizes that his thoughts are already somewhere else and that his indifference unmistakably accounts for his exceptional, almost excessive politeness.

Can any of them, any of my benevolent friends and concerned Western politicians, any of those journalists who curse their bad luck for having to report from a country where there is no simple, clear-cut division into good guys and bad, can any of those people understand how it feels to be going back to the unknown: the nausea, the cramp in the stomach, the agonizing sensation of being overwrought, ill, depressed? I only know what to expect in my own home – hysterical ringing of the phone, unpaid bills, friends with whom I can talk about one thing only, because everything else seems inappropriate, because everything personal has been wiped out, and endless news, news, news ... Everything else is a frightening uncertainty. When the roads are blocked and railways, shops and cars are being blown up, when Serbs from Slavonia are fleeing across the Danube into Voyvodina on ferries and the Croats may be using the same ferries to flee to this side, when the village of Kijevo in Croatia is isolated and the Federal Army blocked at Lištica, all plans and all thoughts about the future (holidays, summer vacations, travel) become pointless. I feel that for all of us the future is being gradually suspended and this seems to be the most dangerous thing. The irrational that dwells in each of us is being unleashed from its chain and nobody can control it any more. Nobody is secure. In what way am I, a Croat, less threatened and in less danger than my acquaintance, a Serbian, who is now moving back to Eastern Bosnia? In no way, because the demons in us have already made people perceive themselves as nothing but parts of the national being. 'The Serbs must be slaughtered,' says a twelve-year-old child from my neighbourhood playing with the bread-knife. His mother slaps his face, while the other grown-ups around the table lower their eyes, aware that they are to blame for his words. The boy, of course, is only playing. At the same time, children his age in Belgrade are probably not playing cops and robbers any more – they are also playing at what should be done to Croats. If there is any future at all, I am afraid of the time to come. A time when these boys, if this lasts, might do just that.

ZAGREB
APRIL 1991

2

MY FATHER'S PISTOL

Everyone here says that we are at war now, but I still hesitate to use this word. It brings back to mind my father's Beretta pistol that he brought home with him after World War II. Why did he show it to me and my brother when we were only nine and five years old? I suppose because it would be dangerous if we found it on our own. I remember how he took it from the top of an old oak cupboard in the bedroom, and unwrapped it from its soft white cloth. He took the pistol in his hand with a strange expression, then allowed us to hold it for a moment. It felt heavy and cold. Pretending that I was playing, I pointed it at my little brother. 'Boom-boom!' I wanted to say, but when I looked at my father's face I froze. He was as white as a sheet, as if in that instant he had recognized a familiar phantom, a long forgotten ghost of war. He took the Beretta from me. 'Never,' he said, 'not even in a play, do that again. Don't touch weapons. Remember, sooner or later guns bring death. I ought to know, I've been through the War.'

My father joined Tito's partisan army in 1942, when he was twenty, and this was one of the very few occasions he ever mentioned the War. He was not of the kind to tell anecdotes, slightly changing them each time to make him look the hero. Years later when I had grown up and asked him about this strange silence, a blind spot in his biography, he told me that war was the most horrible thing a human being can experience and that we, his children, didn't need to know what it looked like. It wouldn't happen again. He fought so it wouldn't happen ever again. If it wasn't for his Beretta and a couple of photographs showing a tall blond man in a shabby partisan uniform, I wouldn't have known he'd ever been in the war. But he did say that the War changed the entire course of his future. He had wanted to become a sailor, a sea captain perhaps. To travel, to see the world. I used to imagine him in a white uniform standing on the ship's bridge, and thought that he would have made a handsome young captain. The brutal disruption of the tender fabric of his life, this is what he regretted deeply, the way a war snaps your life in half yet you have to go on living as if you are still a whole person. But, as I learned from his example, you are not – and never will be – a whole person again.

I hesitate to use the word war, which has recently become tamed and domesticated in our vocabulary like a domestic animal, almost a pet. It reminds me of typical Yugoslav movies from the fifties and sixties, war movies about Tito's partisans like 'Kozara' or 'Sutjeska' where the most famous battles against the Germans were fought. Our post war generation was raised on this sort of movie, on the cliché of blond, cold-eyed cruel German Gestapo officers or soldiers (a role usually played by the same actor in most of the films), of bloodthirsty troops from the Serbian ex-royal army, the Chetniks, or of savage Croat Nazis, the Ustashe. On the other side were the brave, intelligent, humane partisans, always victorious, shouting 'Hurrah, comrades!' in the mass battle scenes. Soon we discovered, more by intuition than by comparison – because at that time, in the early sixties, there were few foreign movies to compare ours to – that this scheme things was pathetically simple. So we began to assume an ironic attitude towards the War, to the partisans and the communist revolution – to our history as represented in such caricature. We believed that it all belonged to the past. However, despite our irony, one idea lingered in our subconscious, the idea of a war for freedom, the idea of defending your homeland. In other words, even for the post-war generation in Yugoslavia, the War was not a futile and senseless blood-letting but on the contrary a heroic and meaningful experience that was worth more than its one million victims. This idea was hard to challenge because our whole education – lessons, textbooks, speeches, newspapers – was impregnated with it as if our history prior to 1941 barely existed. And it stays with us still.

But war is not a single act, it is a state of facts and minds, a head-spinning spiral of events and a gradual process of realization. And even if my father had attempted to explain, it wouldn't have been any help to me now because it seems that everyone has to learn this truth alone, step by step, from the events of his or her own life. War is a process: we, in Yugoslavia, are now witnessing this. That is why it is hard to say when it started, who started it and who exactly is the enemy. It hasn't been declared yet, there is no formal beginning such as one country handing another a note. On the one hand, it is clear that the beginning is rooted in political plans and concepts that preceded the war, as well as in the readiness of people to accept measures that would give rise to nationalist tensions – for example, the treatment of the Serbian minority by the new Croatian government before they started causing real problems. On the other hand I may be wrong in saying this, in blaming people at large. After forty-five years under communist rule, no matter how different or more lenient it was than in other Eastern bloc countries, one has no right to claim that people should have been aware of the consequences that nationalism – the tendency to form nation-states – would bring. They had simply had no chance to become mature political beings, real citizens ready to participate, to build a democratic society. When people in Croatia held the first free multiparty elections in 1990, as in most of the rest of East Europe they voted primarily against the communists. Despite that, the new governments were all too ready to proclaim themselves the sole bearers of democracy, as if it were a fruit or a gift there for the taking. If there is any reason at all behind the historical animosities dividing the Yugoslav nations, it is that this society never had a proper chance to become a society not of oppressed peoples, but of citizens, of self-aware individuals with developed democratic institutions within which to work out differences, conflicts and changes and instead of by war. Continuing to live with the same kind of totalitarian governments, ideology and yet untransformed minds, it seems the people were unable to shoulder the responsibility for what was coming – or to stop it. War therefore came upon us like some sort of natural calamity, like the plague or a flood, inevitable, our destiny.

The beginning of war lies not only in political events, not only in the build-up of hatred, but in the way the first images of death stick in your mind and stay there forever tinged with the deep crimson hue of gore. It was in late April, right after Easter when I saw a black and white photo of a man lying on his back, hands stretched above his head with his jacket yanked up

13

because someone had been dragging him by the feet, his body leaving a long dark trace in snow that hadn't melted. His dead eyes were wide open, reflecting a little spot of pale sky above him – the last thing he saw. This was the first front-page picture of a dead man in what would soon become known as the 'first Croato-Serbian war'. His name was printed on the cover too: Rajko Vukadinović. Less than three months later, I saw another photograph, almost identical, but this time the dead man had no name, he had become just a corpse. With a hundred dead in Slavonia, Banija and Krajina, nobody's name matters any more – even if printed it will soon be forgotten.

Yet another photo frames the transitional period in which everything changed – not merely because of the growing numbers of dead or wounded, but because of Slovenia. That is where the war was first announced: by the Federal Army against its own people, by Serbs against the rest of the Yugoslav republics, by Croat extremists, by illegal militia from Krajina. This war doesn't have only two warring sides. It is many-sided, nasty and complex – a dangerous civil war that threatens to change the face of Europe. There is yet another photo that I can't get out of my mind, of a young soldier shot in an army truck, his head dangling out of a side window, a stream of dried blood dribbling out of his ear. He's no more than nineteen. As I think of him, I am afraid that this is the picture of our future.

When I look around me, I see that the war is happening to my dentist, who is afraid to let his children go to his summer house on the islands because he can't be sure they won't be stopped, robbed or taken hostage. 'I hate it,' he says, 'the Serbs have turned me into a fierce Croat nationalist, a thing I was sure would never happen to me.' My friend Andreja is leaving for a village and is planning to sow potatoes, cabbages, and so on. She is a young university professor who should be working on her doctorate this summer; but she can't write or read any more, all she can do is listen. Then Mira calls. The other day, when she was travelling by train from Subotica to Belgrade, there were a dozen young Serbs on board. 'The lady is reading a book in the Roman alphabet?' they sneered spotting the book in her hands. 'Surely the lady must be Croat. How about a nice fuck, you bloody bitch? Or you would prefer this?' one asked, sliding the edge of his palm across her neck, as if he was holding a knife. 'I could be his mother,' she told me, her voice cracking. When I last visited my Serbian friend Žarana in Belgrade a month ago, I jokingly said that I was reserving her cellar as a hiding place. 'I will be your Jew,' I said. But she was serious. 'Don't make such cruel jokes. You know, I really feel like a white communist in South Africa, I am a traitor here.' Another friend in Zagreb decided to give up listening to the radio, watching TV or reading newspapers. He cut himself off from all information, all news. At first I thought it was mere escapism to decide to ignore the war, as if it had nothing to do with his own life. But now I see it was his last, desperate attempt at staying normal, because the war had already poisoned his existence, and there was nothing he could do about it. Rada is a Croat living half in Zagreb, half in Belgrade, married to a Moslem: she is thus a Yugoslav, a rare bird indeed in this time of nationalist divisions. She tells me that she has heard from a very reliable source that the war will last six days. A six-day war, and someone already knows this? Then someone else is telling me that it will start in Croatia on 28 July. Now, the date is known in advance? But I know that this – as well as anything else – is possible, because here rationality simply doesn't exist any longer. Why do I stay here, I keep wondering, as if there is an easy answer to that question. Or as if I have somewhere else to go.

While I shop for dog food in a store selling hunting equipment, where they also sell guns, an old man comes in offering to sell a lady's pistol for 1000 DM. He puts it down on the counter, small and shiny like a silver toy. All of a sudden, I felt a strong urge to possess it, to buy it, to have it – me, too. Why not, I think, I am alone, defenceless and desperately frightened. My desire only lasts a second, but I realize that in that moment the jaws of war have finally closed around my fragile life. Then the image of that photo surfaces, of the dead boy soldier. And of my father, holding his Beretta. They merge into one. Leaving the shop, I start to cry. Like my father's, my life now is breaking in two.

ZAGREB
JULY 1991

3

A BITTER CAPPUCCINO

I'm sitting in a café on Duke Jelačić Square in Zagreb. It is a pleasant, warm mid-July afternoon and a waiter is cranking out the yellow awning to protect us from the sun. The bamboo chair has a soft, pink cushion, the tablecloth is neat and my cappuccino a little bitter, the way I like it. In the concrete vases edging the café they have planted roses – this year, I think – while the sun gleams on the marble pavement as if it was just another Thursday, another perfectly ordinary summer day. Perhaps a month ago I would even have said that it was. But events over the last three weeks in Slovenia have changed our lives and our whole perception of reality. Suddenly I recognize signs, scenes and signals of that changed reality all around me that I hadn't noticed before – or had noticed, but pretended they didn't matter – and they are telling me we are at war.

On the front page of a newspaper lying next to my cappuccino, there is a note from the Red Cross. It's short and impersonal, giving information on the dead, wounded or captured in Slovenia: 39 Federal Army soldiers, 4 territorial defence soldiers, 4 policemen, 10 civilians and 10 foreign citizens, all dead; 308 wounded and 2539 prisoners of war. As I

17

read it over and over, this list of nameless, faceless people summed up together in numbers, it feels like a final sentence, proof that what we are living and experiencing now is something different, unprecedented. More than pictures of tanks pounding through cars and barricades, or of the frightened faces of young soldiers lost in action, the anonymity of this number means that war has been declared. All last year war was a distant rumour, something one managed to obscure or ignore – something happening to other people, to people in Knin or Slavonia on the outskirts of the republic, but never to us in the centre, in Zagreb. We were busy with our private lives, with love, careers, a new car. War was threatening us, but not directly, as if we were somehow protected by that flickering TV screen which gave us a feeling of detachment – we might just as well have been in Paris or Budapest. For a long time we have been able to fend off the ghost of war; now it comes back to haunt us, spreading all over the screen of our lives, leaving no space for privacy, for future, for anything but itself.

Not far from the café I notice people gathering around a taxi to listen to the news. The volume is turned up high, the small group listens in silence to news of the latest manoeuvres of the Yugoslav Federal Army as the speaker's voice echoes across the half-empty square. For these people, as for me, war is not only a state of affairs, but a process of gradual realization. First one has to get used to the idea of it. The idea then has to become part of everyday life. Then rules can change, rules of behaviour, of language, of expectations. The speaker first reads an army communiqué, then a declaration (one of many) of the Croatian President, Franjo Tudjman, about the need to defend ourselves. In this type of discourse, there is no room for dialogue any more, but only for opposing sides to issue warnings, threats, conditions . . .

I remember with vivid clarity the details of the last few days. In a grocery store, I overheard a woman reading a long shopping list to a salesman: 16 litres of oil, 20 kilos of flour, 20 kilos of sugar, 10 kilos of salt, canned beans, rice . . . Are these measurements an indication of how long this war is going to last? And how would I know what to put on such a list, how to compose it? The assistant loaded the provisions into cardboard boxes, then took them to the woman's car. Later on, he tells me that the other day they sold three truck loads full of flour. 'It all started when Slovenia was occupied,' he says. With a pretence at normality, I buy bread, fruit, milk, the usual things. I don't want to be part of this hysteria, I think. But once at home, I call my mother to ask whether she remembers anything about stocking up for the War? What should I buy? She hesitates a little, not because she doesn't remember – she does – but because such a precise question confronts her with the new reality of our lives. Then she recites: oil, flour, salt, candles, potatoes, bacon, sausages, pasta, rice, tea, coffee, soap . . . 'But I don't have a place to store it,' I tell her in despair. 'You have to make room, store it in your bedroom,' she says, as if it is normal by now to keep potatoes where you sleep. 'And don't forget salt!' she adds, in a tone of voice that makes me think that salt is likely sometime to save my life, even if I don't at the moment understand exactly how. Last year, when a friend told me that she found some salt in her cellar that her grandma had stocked there during the last war, I hooted in disbelief. Now I wouldn't laugh.

There is still an impulse to ignore the war, to lead your own life. I see it in my friends planning to go to the coast (but roads are dangerous, last night a train was shot at, and airports might close at any moment). On the other hand, as my daughter pauses a little before packing her suitcase for a holiday in Canada, 'Shall I take only summer things? Perhaps, some light autumn clothes, too?' she asks me, as if not sure how long it will be before she comes back. In her question, I recognize war creeping in between us, because the real question behind her words is: am I coming back? But this question is unspoken, because we are not able to face the fact that we might not see each other for a long time. Instead, she writes out instructions for me about what I have to see to for her at the University where she is a student of archeology. But while she is packing, I notice at the bottom of her suitcase a little shabby grey dog, her favourite toy. I hold my breath for a moment, pretending not to see it. How does one recognize the beginning of it all, I wondered not long ago. Now I see the answer in a tiny padded dog packed away among my daughter's belongings: the war is here, now.

A few weeks later, returning from a short visit to London, I hear a girl next to me, no older than twelve, say to her friend as the aeroplane flies over Croatia: 'If we were forced to land in Zagreb, I would have to lie about my Serbian nationality, or those Croats would kill me on the spot.' We are all trapped. The two girls are at war, too: and even if hostilities were to cease instantly, how long would it take for these girls not to be afraid of landing in Zagreb?

The other night in Zagreb Ana called me from Berlin where she managed to escape while Ljubljana was bombed, telling me that her five-year-old daughter, hearing the sound of a distant aeroplane, asked her: 'Are they going to bomb us here too?' How long will it take Ana's little daughter to forget the sound of a military airplane attack.

While I wait at a tram stop near my house in Zagreb, an ordinary-looking man, a civilian in a light summer suit, opens his jacket for a moment and I can see that he has a pistol tucked in his belt. The tram comes and we get on. But I have this uneasy feeling that my future is in his hands and there is no way to step down off the tram any more.

ZAGREB
JULY 1991

4

DEAD SILENCE OF THE CITY

I took my documents, my computer, and with my two dogs I left Zagreb. It was a bright autumn day, Tuesday 17 September, the third day after the war in Croatia had finally reached us, its capital city. It was here – after months and months of dread, guessing, hearing the fighting getting closer and closer, the fear escalating. We thought, for no good reason, that it couldn't happen, not in Zagreb. Zagreb was somehow different from Vukovar, Osijek, Petrinja or even the ancient cities on the Adriatic coast of Split or Šibenik or Zadar. It is not only a city of almost a million people, but the capital city coordinating the life of the entire republic. We believed its huge organism couldn't be destroyed so easily, its vital functions blocked, its tissue torn apart; though we saw the bombing of Osijek, we couldn't have imagined how exposed and vulnerable any city could become.

The previous Sunday had been calm, a little humid. Leaves on the big chestnuts trees along my street were getting a brown rim that looked like rust, a rust hinting at early winter frosts. I invited my friend Sanka to lunch and laughed when she entered my house carrying a little bag with documents, warm clothes, biscuits and a bottle of water, just as the Territorial Defence people had been instructing us to do, in case we had to hide in shelters or cellars during an air-raid. I prepared *pasta al bianco*, opened a bottle of red Cabernet and just as we were about to eat, we heard the strange, unnerving sound. I remember looking at my fork half way down to the plate, holding it there for a long moment as if something, some unknown force, was stopping me from putting it down. Only then did we hear the air-raid alarm – a long howling sound that until that moment we only knew from TV reports. I knew what we were supposed to do – run to the nearest shelter and hide. Instead, both of us sat at the kitchen table listening to the roar of the MIGs flying low overhead. It was not fear that I felt, or panic. Nothing. There was no trace of emotion in me. Instead, I felt an empty space opening up like a hole in my chest, and with each passing moment my legs grew heavier and heavier, as if they were turning into stone. In my mind, I saw one image, a picture that I'd seen in one of the countless war reports on TV. It was a house without a roof. A camera first showed it from the outside – a newly-painted low building – then entered a bedroom. There were two beds complete with blankets, pillows, sheets and so on, even the curtains were still on the windows with the broken glass. But the roof was missing, as if someone had forgotten to put it there or had simply taken it off like a child's toy. Only a few remnants of bricks and a fine dust all over the room showed that the roof had in fact once existed – perhaps only a couple of hours before that picture was taken. The picture of this bedroom with two neat beds, helpless and exposed, looked like a picture from my own life: the perversity of war stripping away from us all intimacy. The war was in my mind, in my legs, on the table, in the plate of pasta getting cold.

Numb, Sanka and I sat there waiting. For bombs to fall. Or for the alarm to stop, whatever. At that point, I understood exactly the meaning of destiny. It is when you know that this is it: there is no choice any more, no solution, no escape, and you are not even horrified, not even tempted to resist, but just ready to take whatever the next moment brings. Even if it brings death.

After about an hour, the alarm over, the city sank into darkness. An enormous power, the power of war, turned off the lights in all the city's windows and streets. That first evening of complete blackout reminded me of a power shortage five or six years ago, when we had to conserve electricity and spent every second or third afternoon with a candle, wrapped in the night as in a soft black velvet shawl. That Sunday night there were still a few cars passing through the empty streets and their headlights looked like the big eyes of wild animals chased by unseen predators. When I looked up at the sky I didn't see stars. It was dark. And for the first time the thought crossed my mind, that the sky now was the enemy too.

On Monday there were two more air-raid alarms. The first time I was in the middle of the city, near the open market. An old man, seeing people running, asked me if an alarm had gone off, but when I answered yes he continued to walk down the street, with the slow pace of someone who was just curious about all the fuss. I went into the first building, then went downstairs looking for a cellar to hide. The staircase was damp, moss covering a wall near the steps. Old electricity wires and gas pipes were creeping down it like snakes, their black skin peeling off in patches. The air was heavy with the smell of moisture, boiled potatoes and cabbage stew: someone lived there. In a long, damp corridor on the left, I noticed a door ajar.

When I came nearer, I saw a murky room with a small window high up under the ceiling. The door opened wide and a young woman with a child in her arms said, 'Come in, please.' But I stayed at her doorstep, motionless. Perhaps the fact that the 'shelter' was the place where she lived every single day of her life, that the 'safe place' deep under ground was in fact her apartment, was what stopped me from entering. I went back up to the street and walked home through the empty city, thinking of her. She didn't need war to be forced underground, she was there already.

I was in my room when I heard the second air-raid alarm in the late afternoon. I switched off the light and in the semi-darkness I stared at the tiny little flowers painted on Laura Ashley wallpaper. I had bought it in London at the beginning of July when the Yugoslav Federal Army dropped the first bombs on Slovenia. I had been wanting to redecorate my bedroom for ages, but went to buy the paper only after I heard the news about the attack. While looking through different samples in a luxurious shop on King's Road, I knew that, in a way, it was a stupid, absurd thing to do just at the moment when entire buildings were being burned out and destroyed. At the same time I was aware that I was doing it in spite of the war, perhaps as a symbolic gesture of faith in a future when putting up new wallpaper would make sense. I still had some hope that the war would soon end.

Now three months have passed; the war in Croatia goes on and on, more merciless and cruel with each passing day. No one can stop it gripping the whole country, clutching even Zagreb, I thought, as I looked at the floral pattern, at the charming little red roses. I wanted to hide, but instead I just covered my head with a blanket. There is no place to hide in Zagreb or any other city. The whole city after all was a place people built to be a hiding place. Its vulnerability therefore is a measurement of our own vulnerability, our own fragility. A wave of helplessness overwhelmed me and I plunged into it as into an immense ocean. Outside, darkness clotted in the city, so solid I could almost bite it. But more than absolute darkness, there was a terrible absence of noise, any kind of noise – of voices, cars, barking dogs, trams, life itself. The city was mute as if, at a single stroke, the million inhabitants of Zagreb had been silenced.

That night I didn't sleep. Alone in the house, in my room, smothered by the heaviness of that unnatural silence, I felt as if I was sentenced to be buried alive: the iron lid of war coming down over me, closer and closer until there was almost no air left to breathe. If only I could have screamed, I knew I would have felt better. But in the dead silence of that night, the shriek caught in my throat. Like so many others, I was suffering together with the city: our trembling pulse was getting weaker and weaker, our nervous system seizing up, our blood circulation slowing, our eyes blinded, our mouths shut. I knew that after that night, seeing the darkness and hearing the silence of Zagreb as it stood in danger of being bombed to death, nothing could ever be the same, for that city or for me.

In the morning, I left. That was not what I'd intended to do. Moreover, it had nothing to do with personal inclination, my will or my reason. My leaving Zagreb was a purely physical thing, a decision brought about at some deeper level so that I was barely aware of it. As if I was merely some agent for it, my body acted on its own. I didn't think, I just moved around the house with my hands packing, turning off water and electricity, closing windows, locking the door. The movements were mechanical, my voice strange and distant as I explained to my neighbour that I was going away for a few days. She nodded understandingly but we both knew that 'a few days' couldn't have the same, specific meaning any more. As I was leaving, I looked back from the taxi window at the empty road to Ljubljana and in the distance I saw my city getting smaller and smaller on the horizon, almost toy-like. Perhaps this is how they see it – the generals – a toy, an icon on a wide video screen where the bombing is no more than a small bleep from the computer.

In the shameless peace of Ljubljana, only 120 kilometres to the west where the war ended after only ten days, the war in Zagreb and in Croatia seemed remote and unreal like a nightmare, at least for a while. On the Wednesday morning, as I walked across a bridge to the old city, with each step I became increasingly aware of the beauty of its yellow and white façades, its baroque ornaments, its narrow streets paved with cobblestones. Then I heard a church bell. The reality was back, the images of churches and church towers destroyed, burned, shot down with shells – almost sixty of them in towns and villages in Croatia. I saw them falling down slowly, like tall trees, or animals, or human beings. Face to face with the serenity of Ljubljana, the war in Croatia hurt even more.

LJUBLJANA
SEPTEMBER 1991

5

ON BECOMING A REFUGEE

When I entered the tiny apartment on the outskirts of Ljubljana vacated by my friend who had fled to France, at first I felt relieved. The window overlooked a quiet green river, late yellow roses were in bloom in a neighbouring garden and on a wooden table near the entrance someone had left a few green apples. That night I could listen to something that I hadn't heard for a long time, the serene silence of a dormant city sleeping without fear. This is another city, another state, not Zagreb, not Croatia, I kept thinking as if I needed to convince myself that I could relax now, take a deep breath at last. I had left Zagreb temporarily, to give myself a break from the growing feeling of panic, of being caught in a trap. At the same time, I knew perfectly well that I might never go back. The country was at war and I wouldn't be the first one to leave home for a few days only to lose it all and have nothing to go back to.

But for a long time I had refused to leave my home, even to consider such a possibility. For months and months, ever since January, I could hear its noise coming closer and closer, but nonetheless I still chose to ignore it. I know these symptoms of denial by heart now: first you don't believe it, then you don't understand why, then you think it is still far away, then you see war all around you but refuse to recognize it and connect it with your own life. In the end it grabs you by the throat, turning you into an animal that jumps at every piercing sound, into an apathetic being trudging from one side of the room to the other, into the street and to the office where you can do nothing but wait for something to happen, to hit you at last. You learn to breathe in death, death becomes your every second word, your dreams are impregnated by dismembered bodies, you even begin to picture your own end. In the morning you don't recognize your face in the mirror, the sickly grey colour of the skin, dark circles under the eyes and the pupils unable to focus on any one thing for longer than a second. The war is grinning at you from your own face.

The first week in Ljubljana I felt like a guest in a better-class hotel in a familiar nearby city. I had taken a few books that I was determined to read finally after having postponed reading them so many times; there were some people I knew and could sit and talk with. Nonetheless, I was a little uneasy with the language. Of course, Slovenians and Croats understand each other, so it was not a problem of understanding but of something else, of a particular context. I was disturbed by the look people give me when I started to speak in Croatian. In the post-office, in a shop buying bread and milk, at a kiosk buying a Croatian newspaper I constantly had the odd feeling that whoever I addressed was looking down at me as if I was begging, telling me without a word that I was not only a foreigner now – but a very special kind of foreigner. That week on the Ljubljana news I heard that there were 8000 refugees from Croatia in Slovenia, and it was only the beginning. To the people of Ljubljana, I was clearly one of them. Yet my perception of my position was still stubbornly different. It took me some time to realize that I was no guest. There was only one thing that distinguished me from the ordinary holiday-maker, I thought, the fact that I was glued to the TV screen and radio broadcasts – the uneasiness, the hesitation and hunger all at once while I listened or shuffled through the pages of the paper, the dryness in my mouth while I read descriptions of the mounting toll of destruction, and the sudden changes of mood depending on what I had read that day. I was a news addict and that symptom alone would have been enough to brand me an exile. Except that during my first week in Ljubljana I wasn't aware that it was a symptom. I thought that what distinguished me from the rest of them was the fact that I planned to go back home soon. I didn't know that this too is typical.

My first weekend began well. It was a warm blue day, Indian summer. I went to the open market as I would have done in Zagreb on Saturday mornings, trying to maintain the routine of everyday life, because I know it helps. Piles of red pepper, the smell of ripe melons, fragrant honey in small glass jars offered for sale by local peasants, green heads of lettuce, the pungent odour of fish, all gave me a feeling that I was at home there, picking up pears, tasting grapes, touching reality with my hands as if I were privileged, or as if that touch had the power to make me feel alive, present, there.

Returning to the apartment I remembered that I needed to have my shoes repaired, but I didn't know where to find a shoemender, I hadn't passed one. I will have to ask, I thought, seeing that by then I had a new kind of need already and I was not prepared for that. This was not the need of an ordinary visitor, but of a person trying to adapt to a city as one gets used to someone else's coat or shoes as protection from the cold even if they are not comfortable enough. Or as if I had to learn to walk again, only this time forgetting churches and monuments and seeking out instead shoemenders, pharmacies, libraries, discount stores. Perhaps then I realized that I would have to start establishing my life there, or go back home. Soon.

It was on Sunday morning when I finally understood what it would mean to become an exile. I was not yet fully awake when the smell of coffee entered the apartment and gently stirred my nostrils. It was the smell of freshly brewed coffee made in an espresso machine, strong and short, the Italian way. This was just as I used to make it on lazy Sunday mornings, drinking it wrapped in an old pullover over pyjamas while tufts of a milky smog still hung on the hortensias in the garden. Then I heard voices, the voice of a small child asking something and a woman's voice, answering quietly and patiently. Someone turned on a radio, there were more voices, the window above me opened and I saw hands hanging out wet socks, towels and sheets on a clothes line. A penetrating smell of roasted meat and chocolate cake, a sound of cartoons and children laughing. I looked around 'my' apartment: except there was not one thing there that was mine. Only a suitcase not yet emptied and my winter coat hanging in the closet with my friend's summer clothes (she took winter clothes with her too), which I had put there hesitatingly, hoping I wouldn't be there in time to wear it because I'd leave before winter, definitely I would. This was not my home, there were no pictures and posters on the walls which I had put there, no books I had bought. There were no dusty book shelves that I was promising myself I'd clean as soon as I had time, nor my daughter occupying the bathroom so I'd have to quarrel with her to let me in. There was no nervous phone ringing together with the sound of a washing machine and a student radio station weaving a fabric of sounds into which I can sink comfortably, because I know it, it is the sound of my own life.

That first Sunday in Ljubljana was empty and white like a sheet of paper waiting for me to write something on it: new words, a new beginning. But I couldn't. My hands were shaking and I didn't know what to write. Living in uncertainty, in constant expectancy of what would come next, I knew I had been deprived of the future, but I could bear it. But until that moment I wasn't aware that I had been deprived of the past too. Of my past I had only memories and I knew they would acquire the sepia colour of a distant, undistinguished event, then slowly dissolve, disappear in the soft forgetfulness that time would bring as a relief, leading me to doubt that I had ever lived that part of my life. The way sun enters my living room in Zagreb, shining on the porcelain cups on the table, the marmalade jar, the butter, the rye bread. The feeling of a wooden staircase under bare feet. The cracking sound in the wall before I fall asleep. My daughter's rhythmic breathing upstairs, a dog scratching in his basket. Security. Suddenly, in the Ljubljana apartment, I felt as if I had woken up with my hands and legs amputated. Or worse still, as if I was standing naked in the middle of the room, my skin peeled off, stripped of everything meaningful, of sense itself. I didn't know what I was supposed to do about it, I just didn't know.

That evening as I walked along the river an old man passed me by, then returned. 'I saw you coming with your suitcase the other day, I live in the building opposite yours. Where are you from?' he asked me. When I told him I was from Croatia his tone of voice changed instantly. 'I've read in the newspapers

32

that you refugees are getting more money per month from the state than we retired people do, and I worked hard for forty years as a university professor for my pension. Aren't we Slovenes nice to you?' The irony in his voice was already triggering a surge of anger in me. I felt an almost physical need to explain my position to him, that I am not 'we' and that 'we' are not getting money anyway. I think I have never experienced such a terrible urge to distinguish myself from others, to show this man that I was an individual with a name and not an anonymous exile stealing his money. I started to explain to him that I was not what he thought I was, but then I stopped mid-sentence, my anger hanging in the air for the moment, then descending to the wet grass below. That dialogue on the bank of the river had nothing to do with us – him, a university professor from Ljubljana, me, a writer from Zagreb. It was the war speaking through our mouths, accusing us, reducing us to two opposing sides, forcing us to justify ourselves. I walked away. But his two sentences were enough to strip me of my individuality, the most precious property I had accumulated during the forty years of my life. I – no longer me – went to 'my home' that was not mine.

The night was chilly, the river under the three white stone bridges dark and silent. As I stood there, I realized I was in a no man's land: not in Croatia any more, nor yet in Slovenia. With no firm ground beneath my feet I stood at the centre of the city realizing that this was what being a refugee meant, seeing the content of your life slowly leaking out, as if from a broken vessel. I was grateful that the stone under my fingers was cool and rough, that I breathed fresh air and I was no longer terrorized by fear. But at that moment, at the thought of becoming an exile, I understood that it would take me another lifetime to find my place in a foreign world and that I simply didn't have one to spare.

LJUBLJANA
OCTOBER 1991

6

THE BALKAN EXPRESS

Early Sunday morning a mist hovered over the Vienna streets like whipped cream, but the sunshine piercing the lead-grey clouds promised a beautiful autumn day, a day for leafing through magazines at the Museum Kaffe, for taking a leisurely walk along the Prater park and enjoying an easy family lunch. Then perhaps a movie or the theatre – several films were premiering.

But when I entered the Südbanhof, the South Station, the milky Viennese world redolent with café au lait, fresh rolls and butter or apple strudel and the neat life of the ordinary Viennese citizens was far behind me. As soon as I stepped into the building I found myself in another world; a group of men cursed someone's mother in Serbian, their greasy, sodden words tumbling to the floor by their feet, and a familiar slightly sour odour, a mixture of urine, beer and plastic-covered seats in second-class rail compartments, wafted through the stale air of the station. Here in the heart of Vienna I felt as if I were already on territory occupied by another sort of people, a people now second class. Not only because they had come from a poor socialist country, at least not any more. Now they were

35

second-class because they had come from a country collapsing under the ravages of war. War is what made them distinct from the sleepy Viennese, war was turning these people into ghosts of the past – ghosts whom the Viennese are trying hard to ignore. They'd rather forget the past, they cannot believe that history is repeating itself, that such a thing is possible: bloodshed in the Balkans, TV images of burning buildings and beheaded corpses, a stench of fear spreading from the south and east through the streets, a stench brought here by refugees. War is like a brand on the brows of Serbs who curse Croat mothers, but it is also a brand on the faces of Croats leaving a country where all they had is gone. The first are branded by hatred, the second by the horror that here in Vienna no one really understands them. Every day more and more refugees arrive from Croatia. Vienna is beginning to feel the pressure from the Südbanhof and is getting worried. Tormented by days spent in bomb shelters, by their arduous journey and the destruction they have left behind, the exiles are disembarking – those who have the courage and the money to come so far – stepping first into the vast hall of the warehouse-like station. From there they continue out into the street, but once in the street they stop and stare at the fortress-like buildings, at the bolted doors and the doormen. They stand there staring at this metropolis, this outpost of Western Europe, helplessly looking on as Europe turns its back on them indifferently behind the safety of closed doors. The exiles feel a new fear now: Europe is the enemy, the cold, rational, polite and fortified enemy who still believes that the war in Croatia is far away, that it can be banished from sight, that the madness and death will stop across the border.

But it's too late. The madness will find its way, and with it, death. Standing on the platform of the Karlsplatz subway, I could hardly believe I was still in the same city: here at the very nerve centre of the city, in the trams, shops, at 'Kneipe', German was seldom heard. Instead everyone seems to speak Croatian or Serbian (in the meantime, the language has changed its name too), the languages of people at war. One hundred thousand Yugoslavs are now living in Vienna, or so I've heard. And seventy thousand of them are Serbs. In a small park near Margaretenstrasse I came across a carving on a wooden table that read 'This is Serbia'. Further along, on a main street, I saw the graffiti 'Red Chetniks', but also 'Fuck the Red Chetniks' scrawled over it. War creeps out of the cheap apartments near the Gurtel and claims its victims.

I am one of a very few passengers, maybe twenty, heading southeast on a train to Zagreb. I've just visited my daughter who, after staying some time in Canada with her father, has come to live in Vienna. There are three of us in the compartment. The train is already well on its way, but we have not yet spoken to one another. The only sound is the rattling of the steel wheels, the rhythmic pulse of a long journey. We are wrapped in a strange, tense silence. All three of us are from the same collapsing country (betrayed by the tell-tale, 'Excuse me, is this seat taken?' 'No, its free'), but we feel none of the usual camaraderie of travel when passengers talk or share snacks and newspapers to pass the time. Indeed, it seems as if we are afraid to exchange words which might trap us in that small compartment where our knees are so close they almost rub. If we speak up, our languages will disclose who is a Croat and who a Serb, which of us is the enemy. And even if we are all Croats (or Serbs) we might disagree on the war and yet there is no other topic we could talk about. Not even the landscape because even the landscape is not innocent any more. Slovenia has put real border posts along the border with Croatia and has a different currency. This lends another tint to the Slovenian hills, the colour of sadness. Or bitterness. Or anger. If we three strike up a conversation about the green woods passing us by, someone might sigh and say, 'Only yesterday this was my country too.' Perhaps then the other two would start in about independence and how the Slovenes were clever while the Croats were not, while the Serbs, those bastards . . .

The war would be there, in our words, in meaningful glances, and in the faces reflecting our anxiety and nausea. In that moment the madness we are travelling towards might become so alive among us that we wouldn't be able perhaps to hold it back. What if one of us is a Serb? What if he says a couple of ordinary, innocent words? Would we pretend to be civilized or would we start to attack him? What if the hypothetical Serb among us keeps silent because he is not really to blame? Are there people in this war, members of the aggressor nation, who are not to blame? Or maybe he doesn't want to hurt our feelings, thinking that we might have family or friends in Vukovar, Osijek, Šibenik, Dubrovnik, those cities under the heaviest fire? Judging from our silence, growing more and more impenetrable as we approach the Croatian border, I know that we are more than mere strangers – surly, unfamiliar, fellow passengers – just as one cannot be a mere bank clerk. In war one loses all possibility of choice. But for all that, I think the unbearable silence between us that verges on a scream is a good sign, a sign of our unwillingness to accept the war, our desire to distance ourselves and spare each other, if possible.

So we do not talk to each other. The man on my left stares

out of the window, the woman opposite sleeps with her mouth half open. From time to time she wakes up and looks around, confused; then she closes her eyes again, thinking that this is the best she can do, close her eyes and pretend the world doesn't exist. I pick up a newspaper, risking recognition – one betrays oneself by the newspapers one reads – but my fellow travellers choose not to see it. At the Südbanhof newspaper stand there were no papers from Croatia, only *Borba*, one of the daily papers published in Serbia. As I leaf through the pages I come across a description of an atrocity of war, supposedly committed by the Ustashe – the Croatian Army – which freezes the blood in my veins. When you are forced to accept war as a fact, death becomes something you have to reckon with, a harsh reality that mangles your life even if it leaves you physically unharmed. But the kind of death I met with on the second page of the *Borba* paper was by no means common and therefore acceptable in its inevitability: . . . *and we looked down the well in the back yard. We pulled up the bucket – it was full of testicles, about 300 in all*. An image as if fabricated to manufacture horror. A long line of men, hundreds of them, someone's hands, a lightning swift jab of a knife, then blood, a jet of thick dark blood cooling on someone's hands, on clothing, on the ground. Were the men alive when it happened, I wondered, never questioning whether the report was true. The question of truth, or any other question for that matter, pales next to the swirling pictures, the whirlpool of pictures that sucks me in, choking me. At that moment, whatever the truth, I can imagine nothing but the bucket full of testicles, slit throats, bodies with gory holes where hearts had been, gouged eyes – death as sheer madness. As I rest my forehead on the cold windowpane I notice that there is still a little light outside, and other scenes are flitting by, scenes of peaceful tranquillity. I don't believe in tranquillity any more. It is just a thin crust of ice over a deadly treacherous river. I know I am travelling towards a darkness that has the power, in a single sentence in a newspaper, to shatter in me the capacity to distinguish real from unreal, possible from impossible. Hardly anything seems strange or dreadful now – not dismembered bodies, not autopsy reports from Croatian doctors claiming that the victims were forced by Serbians to eat their own eyes before they were killed.

Only on the train heading southeast, on that sad 'Balkan Express' did I understand what it means to report bestialities as the most ordinary facts. The gruesome pictures are giving birth to a gruesome reality; a man who, as he reads a newspaper, forms in his mind a picture of the testicles being drawn up from the well will be prepared to do the same tomorrow, closing the circle of death.

I fold the paper. I don't need it for any further 'information'. Now I'm ready for what awaits me upon my return. I have crossed the internal border of the warring country long before I've crossed the border outside, and my journey with the two other silent passengers, the newspaper and the seed of madness growing in each of us is close to its end. Late that night at home in Zagreb I watch the news on television. The anchor man announces that seven people have been slaughtered in a Slavonian village. I watch him as he utters the word 'slaughtered' as if it were the most commonplace word in the world. He doesn't flinch, he doesn't stop, the word slips easily from his lips. The chill that emanates from the words feels cold on my throat, like the blade of a knife. Only then do I know that I've come home, that my journey has ended here in front

40

of the TV screen, plunged in a thick, clotted darkness, a darkness that reminds me of blood.

ZAGREB
NOVEMBER 1991

7

PARIS—VUKOVAR

It was just before Christmas 1991. I was staying in Paris for a few days and at first I felt as distant from the war as it was possible to be. For two days I neither read the newspapers nor watched the news on television. Still believing it could be done, I tried to immerse myself in a different life, at least temporarily, in order to forget the life I had left behind. But my consciousness was already deeply divided, like a case of permanent double vision and there was no way to change it. Seen like that, Paris looked different, too. I walked down brightly lit streets (the brightness of lights at night that suddenly hurts your eyes) and I could hardly feel my own weight. It seemed to me I was almost floating, not touching the pavement, not touching reality; as if between me and Paris there stretched an invisible wire fence through which I could see everything but touch and taste nothing – the wire that could not be removed from my field of vision and that kept me imprisoned in the world from which I had just arrived. And in that world things, words and time are arranged in a different way. Anything at all would take me back: the bitterness of my coffee, a sort of reluctance to move, a glimpse of shoes in a shop window and then instantly a feeling of futility, remoteness, not belonging. In a Europe ablaze with bright lights getting ready for Christmas I was separated from Paris by a thin line of blood: that and the fact that I could see it, while Paris stubbornly refused to.

Only two years have passed since the Christmas of 1989: the fall of the Berlin Wall, Vaclav Havel, the death of Ceauşescu, the day when I first went to midnight mass with my mother. But I can hardly remember any of that. Between then and now there is nothing, just whiteness, absence. Memories seem to have been blotted out by the burden of the present and everything that has taken place in the meantime appears tiny, distant, too trivial to be remembered. I sit in Marija's kitchen while outside a milky fog smothers everything that is not the war. Marija tells me her war story, about her mother who no longer goes to the basement of the old people's home when the air-raid sirens are sounded in Zagreb, how she can no longer live in Belgrade, about her son who abandoned his studies in Belgrade and came to Paris to avoid being drafted for the war against Croatia. Now she is looking for a job. Her husband keeps the TV on all the time, switching from CNN to Sky News to French news broadcasts. His spare time is spent in trying to catch as many programmes as possible, reading all the newspapers he can get hold of, both Serbian and Croatian, in an attempt to uncover the truth behind the propaganda. Then at night he tosses in his bed unable to sleep. Vukovar has already fallen, Dubrovnik is still under siege, without water and electricity. The phone keeps ringing and it seems that with each new call the number of the dead is rising dizzily. Even in this large Parisian apartment with its period furniture, thick carpets that muffle the sound of footsteps and mirrors in elaborate gilt frames, the war permeates our skin, our hair, our lungs like dust. Even those who have been living here for years cannot detach themselves completely, be truly here. The war is a seed, then a seedling and then a plant growing in each of us.

It was late in the evening of the third day when I finally reached for the newspapers. Marija said, Please don't take this one, please don't, but the magazine had already opened by itself in the centre, on a page with a photograph in colour. Behind a house two people were lying on the ground. A man in a red sweater was lying on his side, his shirt sleeves rolled up above the elbow and one hand thrown over his head as if trying to defend himself from a blow. Next to him lay a woman wearing a blue housecoat with a flowery pattern. She was spread out face down, her hair tangled and her face pressed against the frozen earth. Right next to her head was a crumpled yellow package of Digo instant yeast. She must have dropped it when she fell, as if walking the short distance from the house to the field she had been kneading the empty package in her hand; perhaps only a moment earlier she had added the yeast to the flour to make bread. She did not know she was going to die, no, certainly not. Death caught her in the middle of an unfinished chore. I could not keep my eyes off that package; I was riveted to it as if this was the most important detail in the picture. Or perhaps I did not wish to see the whole picture. Finally I allowed my eyes to slide to the left, to the head of the man in the red sweater. Although the photograph was large enough and in focus, at first I thought that what I saw on his face in profile was a large stain of clotted blood. Subconsciously, I may have refused to understand what I saw as well as the meaning of the scene: the man with his hand thrown above his head was missing almost the entire right side of his head. I closed my eyes, but the picture did not disappear. When I opened them again, the vague stain turned into a gaping skull. I put the magazine aside, then picked it up again and looked at the photograph for a while. I felt death seep into me, flood over me, drag me down and engulf me.

That afternoon I cut my finger and when later that night I was running a bath (believing I had already forgotten the photo) the wound split open again and a few drops of blood fell into the water, tinging it pink. Immediately the picture floated into my mind. The bathroom was large, tiled in old-fashioned ceramic tiles with a garland of flowers running along the border. It was warm and quiet in the apartment. The bath was full and I sat in the water. I knew I was safe in this sleeping house in the middle of Paris, that the war could not reach me from the outside, and yet, sitting there in a bath full of hot water, I was shivering, feeling all of a sudden terribly exposed. A tap above the bathroom sink was leaking and its almost inaudible sound suddenly seemed unbearably loud. Now I remembered how I hadn't folded the magazine and pushed it away, I had turned to the next page as if I could not get enough of death, as if the pictures of it held a weird, morbid attraction, a cathartic quality which would make all other similar pictures that were to follow less horrible. Now I know, I needed to make death bearable, I had to overcome the horror welling up in me. When I turned the page, I saw a larger photograph of the same scene. Next to the older couple – in fact, in front of them in the foreground, there lay a young man in blue worker's overalls. On top of him lay a girl, maybe only a child. She must have been the last one killed; she had fallen clumsily over the hand of the young man who was already sprawled on the ground. Her head was turned towards the bullet-scarred white wall of the house, theirs perhaps. They looked like a family – mother, father, son, daughter. The four dead bodies lay spread out in the backyard, next to scattered garbage – plastic bags, papers, some cans. The head of the younger man was split in half and from the crack through the matted black hair his brains had spilled out onto the thin grass. The photograph was bluish and the reddish pink of the blood-stained brain shimmered in front of my eyes like molten lava. Stuck to it was a tiny yellow leaf.

Only once, years before, had I seen death close up.

My younger brother lies in the mortuary. The slanted rays of the autumn sun fall on the concrete floor by the chrome steel refrigerator with four drawers. Next to it is a stretcher which looks like a makeshift hospital cot. My brother is dressed in a dark blue suit and a white shirt, the same suit he wore at his wedding. I cannot come closer, I cannot see his face, perhaps I don't want to see it. He is barefoot, only his socks on. Why isn't he wearing any shoes, I wonder stupidly, as if that question would somehow refute the fact that he is dead. The mortuary smells of disinfectant, the floor is wet, I can see the legs of a woman standing inside as if watching over him. She is wearing black rubber boots. Someone behind me whispers that they must have stolen his shoes, that's what the folk in the mortuary do, later they sell them to make money. At that point death still has no meaning, I know only that it cannot be grasped, it cannot be understood. One can accept it and go on living with the emptiness, but it is impossible to understand anything beyond the simple and evident fact that someone is gone, that he no longer exists – the fact that my brother was alive only yesterday, I talked to him. He was lying in his hospital bed and talked about boats, how he wanted to go sailing. Yes, I said,

46

when you get well we'll go sailing together. I was telling this to him as much as to myself, unwilling to admit that death existed, pushing it away with words from him . . . from myself.

But his death was normal, acceptable, everyday death of a kind which is part of everyone's life: you have to go on living with it. Death on the photographs from Vukovar is something entirely different, it contains the horror of the intolerable. In the glistening spillage of brains exposed there for everyone to see was something worse than death itself. It was defilement. This was no longer merely a horrible death of two men whose inmost vulnerable being, that deepest core which must never be stripped bare, never touched, now lay on the frost-scorched field. Their smashed skulls cancelled out my own effort to live. The naked brain on the grass is no longer death, horror, war – it eludes any explanation or justification, it makes no sense at all. You ask yourself how it is possible to live in a place where things like that are happening. I know I should have asked myself at this point whether the murdered people were Croats or Serbs and who killed them; perhaps I should have felt rage or a desire for revenge. But as I gazed at the dark gaping hole, at the blood-caked pulp, I only felt an unspeakable revulsion towards humankind. The naked brain is stronger than such questions, it is the evidence that we are all potential criminals, that we don't know each other really and that from now on, if we survive at all, we shall have to live in mortal fear of each other, forever and ever. The naked brain crushes, obliterates us, pulls us down into the darkness, takes away our right to speak about love, morality, ideas, politics, to speak at all. In the face of the picture of a naked brain all human values are simply reduced to nothing.

Sitting in the bath, I looked at my body as if it was no longer mine; more than that, as if I no longer wanted it to be mine or wanted to be part of it. The feet, the nails, the hands. I knew all of that belonged to me, that it was me, but my perception of my own body was no longer the same. On my wrists and on the insides of my arms there was a bluish mesh of veins. It occurred to me that my skin was so thin as to be almost nonexistent. When finally I reached out for the towel, it felt like an alien body moving mechanically, no longer in my control. No, it was not fear of death, I would have easily recognized that. I was familiar with the sudden wild pulse booming in my head and the anguished cramp in the pit of my stomach that would spread through my body till I was petrified. Here, in the bathroom, I felt my own terrible fragility and impotence. I was overwhelmed by a frantic urge to escape from this strange and unreliable body. Something in me rebelled at the thought that this form could be me, this vessel, the other with which I had just lost contact.

It must have been a momentary death of sorts, a revulsion, a recoiling from the body I could no longer feel as mine. Under my hard stare the vessel was torn apart from its contents and if someone had hit me at that moment I am sure I would have felt no pain. I squeezed the cut on my finger as if trying to prove to myself I was still alive. A drop of blood fell on my knee. I smeared it on my skin, making a hole-shaped stain. This body was no longer mine. It had been taken over by something else, taken over by the war. I had thought that the death of the body was the worst thing that could happen in war; I didn't know that worse was the separation of self from the body, the numbness of the inner being, extinction before death, pain before pain. Instinctively I licked the wound on my finger. But it didn't help, the blood continued to ooze.

ZAGREB
DECEMBER 1991

8

OVERCOME BY NATIONHOOD

It was usually on 29 November, Republic Day, or some other national holiday. I remember that as a child I was standing in a long row of Tito's Pioneers. Dressed in blue caps decorated with red stars and with red kerchiefs around our necks, we dutifully waved paper Communist Party flags, chanting 'Long live Comrade Tito! Tito! The party!' – while black limousines drove by. There was another slogan that we used to shout on such occasions, glancing at our teacher, who would give us a sign to start. 'Bro-ther-hood! U-ni-ty! Bro-ther-hood! U-ni-ty!' we yelled with all our might, as if we were casting a spell. These words were like a puzzle to me. What was more natural than to wish a long life to Tito, when not only streets, schools and hospitals but also towns were named after 'the greatest son of our nation'? But slogans about brotherhood and unity sounded a little too abstract. Little did I know about the hate, rivalry and bloodshed that divided people in the Balkans throughout history. Little did I know about history at all. How could I know, when, according to our textbooks, history began in 1941 anyway.

The problem was that we – all the people, not just the

Pioneers – were told to shout slogans and clap our hands but never to question what those words meant. And when I did, it was too late. Brothers started to kill one another, and unity fell apart, as if Yugoslavia were only part of a communist fairy tale. Perhaps it was. Nationalism as we are witnessing it now in the former USSR, former Yugoslavia and Czechoslovakia is a legacy of that fairy tale. And it is so for at least three reasons: the communist state never allowed development of a civil society; it oppressed ethnic, national and religious beliefs, permitting only class identification; and in the end, communist leaders manipulated these beliefs, playing one nationality against another to keep themselves in power for as long as they could. Even if the price was war.

I have to admit that for me, as for many of my friends born after World War II, being Croat has no special meaning. Not only was I educated to believe that the whole territory of ex-Yugoslavia was my homeland, but because we could travel freely abroad (while people of the Eastern-bloc countries couldn't), I almost believed that borders, as well as nationalities, existed only in people's heads. Moreover, the youth culture of 1968 brought us even closer to the world through rock music, demonstrations, movies, books and the English language. We had so much in common with the West that in fact we mentally belonged there.

Some of my foreign friends from that time cannot understand that they and I have less and less in common now. I am living in a country that has had six bloody months of war, and it is hard for them to understand that being Croat has become my destiny. How can I explain to them that in this war I am defined by my nationality, and by it alone? There is another thing that is even harder to explain – the way the awareness of my nationality, because of my past, came to me in a negative way. I had fought against treating nationality as a main criterion by which to judge human beings; I tried to see the people behind the label; I kept open the possibility of dialogue with my friends and colleagues in Serbia even after all telephone lines and roads had been cut off and one-third of Croatia had been occupied and bombed. I resisted coming to terms with the fact that in Croatia it is difficult to be the kind of person who says, 'Yes, I am Croat, but . . .'

In the end, none of that helped me. Along with millions of other Croats, I was pinned to the wall of nationhood – not only by outside pressure from Serbia and the Federal Army but by national homogenization within Croatia itself. That is what the war is doing to us, reducing us to one dimension: the Nation. The trouble with this nationhood, however, is that whereas before, I was defined by my education, my job, my ideas, my character – and, yes, my nationality too – now I feel stripped of all that. I am nobody because I am not a person any more. I am one of 4.5 million Croats.

I can only regret that awareness of my nationhood came to me in the form of punishment of the nation I belong to, in the form of death, destruction, suffering and – worst – fear of dying. I feel as an orphan does, the war having robbed me of the only real possession I had acquired in my life, my individuality.

But I am not in a position to choose any longer. Nor, I think, is anyone else. Just as in the days of brotherhood-unity, there is now another ideology holding people together, the ideology of nationhood. It doesn't matter if it is Croatian, Serbian, Czech, Slovak, Georgian or Azerbaijani nationhood. What has happened is that something people cherished as a part of their cultural identity – an alternative to the all-embracing communism, a means to survive – has become their political identity and turned into something like an ill-fitting shirt. You may feel the sleeves are too short, the collar too tight. You might not like the colour, and the cloth might itch. But there is no escape; there is nothing else to wear. One doesn't have to succumb voluntarily to this ideology of the nation – one is sucked into it.

So right now, in the new state of Croatia, no one is allowed not to be a Croat. And even if this is not what one would really call freedom, perhaps it would be morally unjust to tear off the shirt of the suffering nation – with tens of thousands of people being shot, slaughtered and burned just because of their nationality. It wouldn't be right because of Vukovar, the town that was erased from the face of the earth. Because of the attacks on Dubrovnik.

Before this war started, there was perhaps a chance for Croats to become persons and citizens first, then afterwards Croats. But the dramatic events of the last twelve months have taken away that possibility. Once the war is over – and I hope the end is near now – all the human victims will be in vain if the newly emergent independent countries do not restore to us a sense that we are before all else individuals as well as citizens.

ZAGREB
JANUARY 1992

9

THE SMELL OF INDEPENDENCE

I was sitting in a car and through a windshield, down the road, I could see a roadblock with a yellow sign DOUANE and a policeman looking at someone's passport, then waving them on. On the right side of the road there was a white metal house, like a trailer – a police and customs station – and on a high mast beside it fluttered the new Slovenian flag. It looked like an improvised check-point in some remote province, except that it was supposed to be a main check-point between Slovenia and Croatia and I was crossing it for the first time. The border was brand new too; the Croats hadn't even had time to post a guard on their side. I got out of the car. Standing on a piece of asphalt in Bregana, bathed in a weak winter sun, I slowly reached for my passport and handed it to a Slovenian policeman, a young man who approached me, smiling, as if proud of what he was doing. I looked at my passport in his hands. It was the old red Yugoslav passport, of course. All of a sudden I became aware of the absurdity of our situation: I knew that, while he inspected my Yugoslav passport, he must still carry the very same one. There we were, citizens of one country falling apart and two countries-to-be, in front of a border that is not yet a proper border, with passports that are not good any more.

Until then, the Slovenian state, the Croatian state, borders, divisions, were somehow unreal. Now, these people with guns in Slovene police uniforms stand between me and Slovenia, a part of the country that used to be mine, too. A few weeks ago I was free to go there. Now I cannot. *What would happen if I started to run now?* I thought, suddenly remembering the Berlin Wall. *Would the smiling young policeman shoot me?* Although I was sure that he wouldn't, for the first time I experienced the border physically: it felt like a wall. In that moment, I knew that everything they say about walls coming down in Europe is lies. Walls are being erected throughout Europe, new, invisible walls that are much harder to demolish, and this border is one of them.

At least I could still go to Slovenia, could travel there, even with a passport. I can't go to Serbia. I can't even make a simple phone-call to Belgrade. Perhaps, if I really wished to go there, I could take one train from Zagreb to Budapest, then an overnight train to Belgrade – twenty-four hours of travelling through Hungary, instead four hours on the Intercity train that used to take me direct to Belgrade before the war. But this is not the worst. Going east, there are no more roads, railways, no border; there are only bombed towns, burned villages and piles of corpses no one has had time to bury. What should be the eastern border of Croatia is nothing more than an open wound.

The last time I visited Belgrade was in July, after the Yugoslav Federal Army had attacked Slovenia. As I listened to the news in a taxi from the airport, a speaker said something about an army 'victory' there. 'See!' the taxi driver said with a triumphant smile, as if this was his personal victory. He didn't know where I came from. I didn't say a thing, I didn't dare. His comment might have been casual and innocent, his triumphant smile a small and unimportant gesture, but it paralysed me with fear. The essence of war was there, growing silently between us.

The mistrust was palpable in the thick dusty air of Belgrade last summer. People from different republics couldn't talk to each other any more, they stopped trusting. I didn't like it then, that uneasy feeling of a country shrinking, being eaten by hatred, a country virtually disappearing under my feet. But I didn't realize that it was going to be amputated in such a painful way. Not only land, but friends were cut off from each other, too. Friendships could hardly survive this war. Could they survive questions like: what did you do in the war? Could we address each other as individuals, or has this possibility been taken from us for the next twenty years? After the war the roles will be reversed and the victims will judge not only the executioners, but their silent accomplices. I am afraid that, as we have been forced to take sides in this war, we – all of us, on both sides – will get caught in that cruel, self-perpetuating game forever, even against our will, and I have no way of knowing if my friends are aware of this yet. If I ask them that question, I make myself into an inspector of their consciences, their souls. If I don't, I am a hypocrite. But even if they pass this stern test, there remains the divisive fact of war itself – the experience of it, the way it has changed our lives. The fact that my (and their) friend is wounded, another still fighting, I don't know where. The fact that a mutual friend's house near Dubrovnik has been burned down. The fact that for a long time I, like everyone around me, didn't know what to do with a word like 'future'; I didn't recognize it, it served no purpose at all. In this war, people have lost words, friends, sons, a sense of life. Even as I write this I hear machine-gun fire nearby. It is 11 pm and I can hear people's voices and cars passing by. No one stops at the sound of shooting. Neither do I. A chilly thought that these shots might mean someone's death is pushed away with the excuse that this is a war. Could my friends in Serbia ever understand how war has become an everyday reality for us – the air-raid alarms, the nervous waiting for news, men in uniforms, dark, empty city streets, blackouts, and a permanent engorging sense of fear, that only grows with each passing day?

My friend in Paris who moved there when she was ten years old, at the end of the Algerian war, told me that her teacher had asked her why, even after years of living in France, she walked down a street zig-zag. This is how you walk to avoid a bullet, she explained to her teacher. And this is what the generation of children who survived a war in Croatia will do, walk zig-zag and run to hide in cellars at the sound of an aeroplane.

But the worst are images, because they don't go away, they stay in your mind and you wake up in the middle of the night sticky with sweat, screaming. Strangely enough, watching it day after day the war teaches you to get used to blood, you are forced to cope with it. After a certain point (which comes very quickly) you realize that people are dying in great numbers and bodies simply pile up like an abstract number on the surface of your mind. In order to survive, you become cruel. You are touched only if you knew the person who died, because in order to comprehend the reality of death you need to identify it, to get acquainted with its face, to personalize it. Otherwise, you feel the pain but it is vague and diffuse, as if you are wearing metal armour that is too tight.

What one cannot escape are images of innocence: children's

faces, a puppy wandering among the charred remains of village houses, a lying dead newborn kitten in a muddy field with its little head strangely twisted, a lost shoe on a sidewalk. On Christmas Day the television reported a particularly fierce attack on the town of Karlovac, some forty kilometres from Zagreb. First the camera showed a distant view of it, with clouds of smoke and dust rising above the rooftops. Then the camera closed in on a street of half-ruined houses and of soldiers picking up a wounded person – so far, it was a fairly average war report unlikely to change the rhythm of one's pulse. Only when the camera zoomed in on a little house with two smouldering black holes for windows, did I feel as if I'd been punched in the stomach. It was a particularly fine day and the burned shell of the house stood outlined against a deep blue winter sky. A little further on, in front of the house, was a clothes line with a man's freshly washed white shirt and women's underwear on it. I could imagine a woman, only a short time ago, standing outside hanging it there. As she returned to the house a bomb fell and everything was over in an instant. The house was in ruins, the people inside had probably been killed. Yet, the shirt and underwear were dangling in a light wind, as if the woman would return at any moment to collect it – clean, dry, smelling of the north wind and distant snow-capped mountains. This was a picture of death itself.

It is January 1992 and by now I know there is no way back. Both borders, the Slovenian and the Serbian one, have taught me my new reality, the fact that I am about to live in a new, a different country with a different shape and a different name: shaped like the core of an apple, and its name incurably associated with blood. However, on the eve of independence (I heard on the news that the European Community is going to recognize Croatia tomorrow, 19 January 1992) I feel ambiguous. I feel robbed of my past, my childhood, my education, my memories and sentiments, as if my whole life has been wrong, one big mistake, a lie and nothing else. I'm a loser, indeed we are all losers at the moment. The Croatian 'new democracy' hasn't brought us anything yet but promises to believe in. The cost is high: renunciation of the whole past and sacrifice of the present.

Croatia has proved two things to the world. First, that the process of self-determination cannot be stopped, and it will be remembered for that. The second lesson, I'm afraid, is that self-determination has no price, and if it has no price it means that a human life has no value. People didn't vote to lose their sons in the struggle for independence, but the independence stinks of death. A sweet, poignant smell of burned soil and rotten flesh saturates the air. It is rising from the battlefield, from roads and hospital rooms, from half-empty cities and deserted villages, from army camps and ditches, from the people themselves. One can sense it even in Zagreb. Going into the post-office or boarding a tram one smells this distinct, familiar odour as if all of us, alive and dead, were marked by it forever.

Then, again, this ambiguity has its positive aspects: in it there lies a hope for the war's end. There is a new kind of pride, too. Two years ago, if you mentioned that you came from Croatia (which you probably wouldn't mention anyway, because you knew it wouldn't make sense to a foreigner) people would look at you in bewilderment repeating the unknown name with a question mark, as if it were a country on another planet, not in Central Europe.

I hope I will love my new country. I know it is a strange

thing to say at this moment of celebration. The presumption is just the opposite: that Croatia is getting its independence simply because millions of people loved it enough to fight and to shed their blood for it practically to the death. But it is not only physically a new country, it is politically a different state and no one knows exactly what life will look like here once the war is over – it could turn into a democracy or a dictatorship, there are no guarantees for either.

When he was elected president, John F. Kennedy in his famous inaugural address to the nation, said: 'Don't ask what the country can do for you, ask what you can do for your country.' To my mind the citizens of Croatia have to ask themselves a very different question. Having already done everything possible for their country, they have the right to ask: 'What will our new country do for us, its citizens? Will the sacrifice of all these lives be worthwhile?'

ZAGREB
JANUARY 1992

10

IT'S HARD TO KILL A MAN

Sisak is a small town less than sixty kilometres from Zagreb. This is the starting point of the front line. A little to the south, across the Sava, is the last southeastern stronghold of the Croatian army. A few days ago the Federal Army shelled the oil refinery, the hospital suffered several direct hits, the church was damaged. From where I'm sitting, near the door, I can see the street and in the street, right in front of the café, a hole made by a rifle grenade. It's a wonder that the café is open at all, I think, for the first time physically aware that the war is close by. A woman is washing up some glasses at the counter. She is wiping them slowly, absent-mindedly, gazing through the window at some frost-bitten pigeons on the pavement across the road. The café is almost empty except for a few men in uniform. They stand leaning with their elbows on the counter and drinking beer. The barmaid and I are the only women in the room; the windows are blacked out with paper and the whole place is permeated with the dull smell of weariness. The front seems to begin at the very table where I'm sitting, as if the war is a sort of mythical animal which you can never properly glimpse, though you feel its scent and the traces of its presence all around you: in the woman's movements, in her look, in the way the uniformed men lean on the counter, tilt the bottles to their lips and then wipe their mouths with the backs of their hands and leave abruptly; in the air of uncertainty which at this moment, for no particular reason, becomes quite palpable.

I sit and wait for my guide to the front to come. The 16 January ceasefire has held for almost a month and this time it seems it will hold, at least for a while; nevertheless, this is as far as you can go unaccompanied. In the undamaged County Hall with its dark-red façade which now houses the Croatian military headquarters and a press office, they told me that the guide's name was Josip and that he was a veteran, meaning that he had been fighting since the beginning of the war in this area. The man who checked my papers and signed a permit said to me – perhaps because I'm a woman – 'I only wish I had a plate of hot soup', as if this sentence would best explain to me how he felt. He might as well have said, I only wish I could get some sleep, or watch a soccer game on TV or have some peace and quiet. Each of his wishes would have been equally pointless. The office was sparsely furnished: an ordnance map of the Sisak region on the wall, a long table and some chairs with metal legs that grated on the floor whenever they were moved. A woman brought in fresh coffee, men in uniforms sitting around the table pored over maps and made notes. As in movies about World War II, I almost expected a moustached commander to stride into the room and for everybody to jump up and salute. The setting was so familiar that for a moment I thought this must be a mistake. No, this cannot be military headquarters, no, this cannot be a real war . . . Leaving the building, I stepped on some grains of rice that crunched under my feet. There must have been a wedding here only yesterday. The thought of a wedding in the midst of war brightened the gloomy mood of the morning.

I have no idea what I expected when I set out for the front. Probably one subconsciously expects to see the same things as on television or in the papers. One expects to experience at least that same level of dramatic tension that the media offer in the process of editing reality: the usual footage of ruins, fires, dead bodies, soldiers, the bewildered faces of civilians, a concentrated picture of suffering. As the media present it, war at some point turns into a pattern, a mould that needs to be filled with content. What we see each night on television is one and the same thing all the time – destruction, death, suffering. Yet, what we see is only the surface. There are so many other layers, invisible ones. Those far from the front lines must wonder how it is possible to endure such pressure day after day, how it is possible to live at all.

Josip arrives. He is of medium height, thickset, with short cropped hair. He is wearing a uniform, but carries no weapons, at least not now. We set off immediately. Josip drives slowly. We pass several military sentries but everything seems peaceful enough, just the soldiers marking time, trying to fend off the cold. On the muddy slope near the ferry which will take us across the Sava river, Josip gets out of the car and says hello to a small group of soldiers who are guarding the ferry. I have trouble coming to terms with the fact that the front is less than an hour's drive away from my home. Less than an hour's drive away and everything is different: dugouts, sentries, the road stretching emptily away before one and an eerie, unnatural silence. Josip is not a talkative man, in any case he seems unwilling to start a conversation. I study his face, his narrow blue eyes, his open smile, his large hands and the unhurried, deliberate way he moves. But his face reveals nothing, it tells me nothing of what the war means to him. I ask him how it all began here. I never thought it would come to this, he says, as if he himself still cannot quite believe that it has come to this. Then he tells me about his neighbour from Sunja who is now fighting on the Serbian side in Kostajnica. His father is a Croat, his mother Serbian and his family has stayed on this side. Josip tells me he has recently seen his neighbour on television passing a message to his own sister that he will cut her throat for marrying a Croat. That's the hardest thing, he says, the treachery of friends and neighbours who were Serbs and who, all but a couple of them (who are still here), left Sunja on the eve of the first assault because they knew that the village was going to be attacked. They left their cattle in the stables, dinners on the table, washing machines spinning. They did nothing to warn their neighbours and friends with whom they had lived side by side for many years. Why did they do it to us, says Josip and shakes his head. There must have been a conspiracy of silence among the Serbs. And the conspiracy of mortal fear. Why did they say nothing? Could they have stayed here? Did Serbian soldiers threaten to kill them if they gave a warning signal to their neighbours, or were the neighbours already the enemy and no threats were necessary? And how will they ever be able to return to these villages? The way Josip talks about this, I can tell that the memories of the betrayal are still fresh.

We enter Sunja. In front of a wooden house a snowman is melting. Most houses in the main street have been hit, the railway station, the former café, the clinic, shops. The street is completely empty, there are no cars or passers-by, no children and no dogs. There are no sand-bags here as in Zagreb, placed to protect shelters and basements; here sand does not help any more. Here and there the holes in the buildings where the doors to the houses used to be are boarded up with planks. There is no glass in the windows, just plastic sheets. Josip laughs, says there are no longer any glaziers here who could repair the windows and it's not worth the trouble anyway. The shelling never really stops so the soldiers distributed plastic sheets for people to stretch over the window frames instead of glass – at least those people who have remained. We come to the church. The parson rides by on his bicycle but does not stop. Emaciated and bowed low over the handlebars, he rides on because the church entrance is locked and the church tower reduced to a heap of rubble. The church clock has toppled from the tower and broken in two. Now the two halves of the clock loom from the debris like two halves of life, split into peace and war. I look at the sky and the ruined eighteenth-century tower of St Mary Magdalen's. Suddenly I realize I am standing in the middle of the cemetery. I look about me at the empty sky, the dead street, the caved-in roof of a house nearby, at the eerie absence of life, the shattered time-piece, and a lump forms in my throat. Standing there, I feel I am approaching an edge, an abyss, a turmoil of feelings which I cannot identify, but know is dangerous, and I know I must stay away from it, because then it would be too late for reason, for doubts, even for fear. While I stand there, everything clicks into place with perfect clarity: they attacked us, we responded. Here, war is a simple matter. There are no politics any more. No dilemmas. Nothing but the naked struggle for life. I know that if I had to stay here, this would soon be my reality too.

I must have been standing in the churchyard for too long,

because my teeth begin to chatter. Josip gently takes me by the arm and leads me down what used to be the main street of Sunja. In the meantime the daylight has turned to dusk and now the darkness is falling swiftly like a curtain. We pass some shops. The glass of the shopwindows lies shattered on the floor and the shelves are completely empty. But on one shelf, the bottom one, I count nine salt cellars made of light-blue china. I stop and count them, I don't know why. Or perhaps I do: because this is the true picture of devastation. There is not a single person in the village who'd buy or even steal the salt cellars, not a single soul who could have any use whatsoever for the salt cellars. Getting into the car, I grow tense, realizing how deceptive the peace and quiet is, as if I can already feel the lurking eyes of the soldiers on the other side.

While we are being ferried across the murky, dark Sava (they tell me that at this very spot they had seen corpses floating on the water), Josip is silent, deep in thought. He told me he was thirty-three years old and was in fact a construction engineer. His face looks quite young and nothing in it reveals his age except two vertical lines cut deep at the corners of his mouth. I don't ask him anything more. Looking at the muddy road in front of us, again I count the blue salt cellars in my mind. Then, quite unexpectedly, I hear Josip's voice saying, No, no, as if he is arguing with himself about things I wouldn't be able to understand anyway. No, he repeats, now looking at me. After the long silence, his words sound strange. I lower my eyes, uncertain whether he is really talking to me. No, the treachery of friends was not the hardest thing, the hardest thing is to kill a man, he says, and uttering those words he stops the car, turns in his seat towards me and looks me straight in the eyes. I stare back at him numbly, I don't think I expected this. Not for a moment since we shook hands and introduced ourselves had it occurred to me that a man who had been fighting for six months must have done it, must have killed someone. I watched him, our shoulders almost touching in the narrow space of the car. I watch his hands on the wheel and feel beads of sweat break out on my forehead. He is saying it, this sentence that no one dares to say out loud in public. The entire horror is compressed in it: war is killing. The sentence hangs in the air between us like a living thing. What hits me at the moment are two things: his closeness and his awareness of what has happened to him. I still cannot quite grasp what he is saying, or perhaps it would be better to say I refuse to grasp it – it is always somebody else who is doing the fighting, not the people we meet, talk with, have coffee with, travel, work or shake hands with.

It was summer, he is telling me, and a few of us surrounded this man, a Chetnik, in a house at the edge of the village. We hid in the tall grass some twenty metres from the house and waited for him to come out. Hours went by, the heat was terrible, but we couldn't move. We knew that any second he would run out of ammunition and then he would try to break loose and bolt. I had gone hunting a couple of times before and at first this felt very much like lying in wait for an animal, no difference. I know that at some point sweat began to pour down my forehead and that I suddenly remembered Camus's *Stranger*. The scene on the beach before he starts shooting at the Arab. *I know,* I thought, *I know that scene. I could almost see Josip there, lying in ambush. He must have licked his salty lips and a blade of grass tickled his neck but he could not move. Then something must have happened in the surrounded house, so his muscles tensed and at that moment . . .* But I did not shoot, continues Josip, nobody did. It was our first ambush and we wanted to be sure we wouldn't miss. I had the best position and sometime around noon I could tell that the man inside was getting edgy, he kept looking out, I often saw him near the windows of the house. At one moment I had him in my sights, I could see clearly his long, thin face surrounded by dark, longish hair. And his eyes, the eyes of a man who knew what was going to happen. I remember that my lips were dry as I squeezed the trigger and I thought, I mustn't miss, I mustn't miss. But I did not pull the trigger. It's hard to kill a man. Next time, next time Josip did shoot and after that there was no going back for anyone. Then Josip says the war made a murderer out of me, because there was nothing else to do but to fight back. The last part of the sentence he says so softly I can hardly hear him.

A girl passes us on the road riding a bicycle. She waves to us. Josip waves back, maybe he knows her. This simple gesture seems to dispel the heavy, sinister shadow cast by his grim words. Fat white geese waddle in the yard of a bombed house we pass. A little farther down the road, a woman is washing the windows of a house with a damaged roof. I can see the notion of war expand to encompass the small, everyday things, from weddings and geese to window washing – the whole, rounded reality. Travelling back to Zagreb, I think how another peaceful day at the front has gone by.

That night, at three o'clock in the morning, Sunja came under fierce mortar attack.

ZAGREB
FEBRUARY 1992

11

MY MOTHER SITS IN THE KITCHEN
SMOKING NERVOUSLY

'What do you think. Will *they* tear his tombstone down?' My mother sits in the kitchen, smoking nervously. It is winter, draughts of cold wind sweep under the balcony door. She talks about Father. In two years since his death her face has changed completely, most of all her eyes. She seems aloof, distant. She has never been close to me, and now I can hardly reach her, except her quite palpable fear. She does not know how to speak of her fear, the words seem to come unstuck from her lips painfully and then, hard and rounded like pebbles, scatter on the table, falling into the ashtray, into the coffee cup which, when she is not smoking, she grips tightly in both hands. I try to catch them, to string them together with the words she is still holding inside herself, because by now she is frightened of their very sound.

Who is she talking about? Who are *they*, who are the people my mother is afraid will demolish or damage my father's tombstone? Every Sunday she goes to the cemetery in the small town on the island of Krk where she was born, about thirty kilometres from the port of Rijeka, where she has lived almost all her life. She usually takes a local bus at ten in the morning and returns at one in the afternoon. She does it regardless of the weather, as if in response to a command. There she cleans the graves of her husband and her son, who died just a month before his father: they are right next to each other. The graves are covered by black marble; dry pine needles and cones drift across them. Then she puts fresh flowers on the graves. From the cemetery she can see the bay. Sometimes she sits and watches the bay and the small town on the hill. But she avoids going up there; rather, she waves down the bus passing near the cemetery and returns home.

I know she does not fear for her son, there is a cross on his grave just like on all but one of the graves – my father's. She is troubled by the red star, the communist one, carved in my father's tombstone. The grave is well out of sight, in a shady spot by the cemetery's northern wall, and the star tiny, almost invisible. But it is the only grave with the star and all the locals know it. She is tormented by the thought. I tell her I don't know whether someone is going to tear it down, it is possible, everything seems to be possible now. And this will have nothing to do with my father being a Federal Army officer – when he died, officers were not yet the enemies of the people, so he died in time – but with the star, the symbol of the former regime and the Federal Army attacking people in Croatia today. I try to imagine the face of the person who might demolish or damage the tombstone, the face of the star-hater. Or several of them. Could it be the local storekeeper, or the young butcher, or the man from the gas station? In the town there are a few fishermen, a dozen or so retired men who bask in the sun by the newsstand like lizards, the Community Centre secretary (what do they call this place now?), an electrician, a harbour master. Otherwise, there are few newcomers, mainly migrant workers from inland. My mother knows them all, she went to school with them. She knows their children and their grandchildren too. My father also knew them, although he came from Rijeka. Every day he used to play cards with them in the taverna, they came to his funeral and afterwards held my mother's hand. Who, then, could do it, I wonder? But at the same time I am aware that the question is pointless. When she says *them*, my mother does not mean anyone in particular. She is not talking about individuals, she is talking about the situation that generates hatred. The war. She is talking about what the war looks like in a small, isolated place on an island where everybody knows everybody, where there are no strangers and people start to search for the enemy in their minds – even a dead one, even symbolic, even carved in stone.

My mother is still nervous, she must have gone through an entire packet of cigarettes by now. She expects an answer from me, but I don't have one, I can see that with each day of the war her insecurity is mounting and *they* are multiplying, becoming even more distant and anonymous. *They* won't give her Father's pension; this has been going on for months. The fact that he had died before the war started and that he was a Croat – so is my mother, incidentally – makes no difference. For the time being, the retired Federal Army personnel, and their widows as well, will not be given their pensions. There are promises that the new government will regulate the matter. She no longer knows what to expect: maybe she will be evicted from her apartment, the apartment is army-owned, in an army-owned building. In the autumn of 1991 when the first air-raid sirens were sounded, the rumour spread that the snipers hiding in the army apartment buildings shot civilians in the streets. The papers claimed that there were about 2500 snipers in Zagreb. Although never officially confirmed, and even denied a month later, this piece of information was carried by all the newspapers with a maddening conviction which left no margin for doubt, almost to the point of proclaiming a lynch-law. At that time most active Federal Army officers, particularly those of other nationalities, had already left Croatia (or transferred to the Croatian army). People moved into their empty apartments at will until the government took control of them. The tenants who remained in such buildings lived as if under siege, waiting for an ominous knock on the door. Their children were scared of going outside to play or of going to school. Now my mother is afraid that she will be evicted, she trusts no one, keeps listening to the news, chain-smokes and has trouble sleeping. The war is everywhere and is different for each.

'Maybe I should have the tombstone changed before this happens,' she says uncertainly, not looking at me.

Now her voice is soft, as if she is begging me to agree. She can sense my disapproval, perhaps even rage. But what do I know of her fear when she approaches the cemetery, opens the iron gate and treads carefully among the graves with a faltering step. Can I possibly imagine what she feels at the moment when she lifts her eyes to look at Father's grave?

I think of Father often these days. He died of a heart attack when he was sixty-seven. He was worn out by his long illness, near the end even breathing was too much of an effort. He wasn't able to go to or from the haemodyalisis on his own; a hospital attendant would pick him up and carry him all the way to the second floor, he was so light. On sunny days he would sit on a small balcony looking out to sea. We have been told he died like that, looking through the open balcony door in the hospital checkroom. The hospital is high up on the hill, facing the harbour. That day he had just got dressed, he did not complain of any pain as usually. When the cleaning woman entered the room, she found him kneeling against a sofa with arms spread, his face turned to the sea. The last thing he saw were the ships on the sun-lit expanse of the sea.

During my rare visits in the last few years, I could hardly recognize his small, wrinkled face which seemed to shrink, as if his skull was beginning to wither while he was still alive. We seldom found anything to talk about. Politics perhaps, but this would invariably start us quarrelling. He was a communist, of 'the idea is fine, only the practice stinks' type. Although Father had grown softer with the years, for me he remained the same rigid man he had always been. The man who got used to pushing people around in the army, the man from whom I ran away from home while I was still practically a child. Standing close to him, I could smell his musty olive-grey uniform which I hated. It was a heavy smell of wool impregnated with the stench of the army canteen, stale tobacco and linoleum, dusty files and the official car. Sometimes, when Mother would iron his uniform over a cloth soaked in water and vinegar it seemed to me I could trace out his entire life in the cloud of steam that billowed from the iron. He went to trade school and loved soccer, bicycling and dancing. In 1942, as a twenty year old, he joined Tito's partisan army. His elder brother was already there, their mother followed them. He fought in the mountains of Gorski kotar, he saw his friends being killed in battle or freezing to death on Matić-poljana. Nobody knows the things he saw. Never, ever, did he speak about the War. Mother has only recently told me that long after the War was over, for five years maybe, he would writhe and sob in his sleep, and then wake up suddenly gasping for air, drenched in sweat, as if he had just dreamed his own death. In their wedding picture he wears his naval uniform; a handsome young man with blond wavy hair combed neatly back. He had to ask permission from the army command to marry my mother, since her family was not 'politically suitable', that is it was a 'class enemy'. And Grandfather and Grandmother were reluctant to give their daughter away to a man in uniform, the uniform which to them meant the uncivilized men from the woods – partisans. Unable to reconcile themselves to the fact that she wouldn't have a church wedding, which was not permitted to an army officer but meant so much to my mother's strong Catholic family, they were to feel resentment to the end of their lives. My grandmother arranged for me and my mother to be baptized secretly; it must have been a kind of revenge. No matter how hard my father tried, he was never good enough for them. The word 'officer' was always spoken with contempt.

Sitting across from my mother, in the place where he used to sit, for the first time I feel close to my father. It is only now that I can grasp the futility of his life, frittered away by history. Like a mirror, it reflects the entire period between the two wars, the last one and the present one, the time when people like him believed that communism was possible. In the mid-sixties he took off his uniform and went to work for a furniture retail company, but he remained a member of the Communist League, believing he owed that much to the party which had transformed the country and pulled it out of poverty and backwardness. Nevertheless, he used to turn off the TV set in the middle of the news programme even before Tito's death in 1980. They've screwed it all up, he would say about his former comrades. His idealism was long gone, the country was falling apart and the communists were refusing to let go of power; that was obvious. Father sat over the spread-out papers and grew old, sinking together with the state he had helped build. He died in the middle of November, 1989, the month and the year that marked the beginning of the final collapse of the communist system. Thank goodness he died – said Mother a couple of months later – this would've been the end of him. For her family, she has been guilty of being his wife; for the communist state, she was guilty of being from another class; and now, when he is dead, she is guilty again. The guilt by relation she had been saddled with in distant 1947 is today still hers to carry. Yet, she cannot understand how her dead husband can possibly be the enemy of the new Croatian state. 'Why did they take my pension away?' she says. 'What will I live on?'

Night falls. It is dark, I can no longer see her face, only the glowing tip of her cigarette. She does not turn on the light. She says it's because of the war, the air-raids, but I know that she is in fact saving electricity. It seems to me Father is here, with us – the man whose past needs to be forgotten now. But he is not the only one: now the time has come to count the dead again, to punish and to rehabilitate. This is called 'redressing the injustice of the former regime'. In the spring of 1990, the monument to the nineteenth-century Croat hero Duke Jelačić, removed by the communist government after World War II and relegated to what was known in the official lingo of the day as the 'junkyard of the past', has been returned to its original place; Republic Square has been renamed after him. The name of the Square of the Victims of Fascism, where once stood the notorious Ustashe prison, has also been changed. The names of virtually all major streets and squares in the cities throughout Croatia have been changed – even the names of cities themselves.

The symbols, the monuments, the names are being obliterated. For a while people will go on remembering the old names, there will be visible traces on the façades marking the spot where the old nameplate was. First the material evidence vanishes, then frail memory gives way. Thus altered and corrected, the past is in fact erased, annihilated. People live without the past, both collective and individual. This has been the prescribed way of life for the past forty-five years, when it was assumed that history began in 1941 with the War and the revolution. The new history of the state of Croatia also begins with war and revolution and with eradicating the memory of the forty-five years under communism. Obviously, this is what we have been used to. It is terrible that this is what we are supposed to get used to again. Even more terrible is that we ourselves tear down our own monuments, or watch it happen without a word, with heads bowed, until a ravaging, 'correcting' hand touches our own life. But then it is too late. In Croatia's 'new democracy', will the past be officially banned again?

Finally, I tell Mother that changing Father's tombstone is out of the question. Every small place has its own, now already official, redesigner of the past who acts in the name of the new historical justice. So far the graves have remained untouched: perhaps the graves will be the sole survivors from the previous system. But if someone indeed intends to remove the star from my father's grave, let him do it by himself, she doesn't have to help. 'Don't change his life, he doesn't deserve it,' I say. 'If it must be, if our past must be blotted out, at least let others do it.' Mother cries helplessly.

RIJEKA
WINTER 1991/2

12

AN ACTRESS WHO LOST HER HOMELAND

I don't know how to begin the story about M, an actress who has lost her homeland in the war. While she sits in an armchair facing me, I cannot help but think how small she looks, smaller than when I saw her last. And quite different from when up on the screen. This is probably always the case with film stars: it is difficult to recognize them because in person they hardly look like the characters they play in the movies. I saw her in Zagreb a year ago at a première of a film: the war had not yet begun, people were celebrating the advent of the new government, the streets were clean, the freshly-painted façades shone in their pretty colours, new shops were being opened, the future looked like a birthday cake with whipped cream and pink sugary icing. M was glowing, people thronged around her and kissed her on the cheeks. She was laughing. She looked happy. That night in the Balkan Cinema foyer, everybody was her friend. And then . . .

The attacks on M began when it came to the attention of the press that she had given a brief, ten-line statement in the bulletin of *Bitef*, Belgrade's international theatre festival. The theatres from Croatia had boycotted the festival held in Belgrade which in the meantime had ceased to be the capital of the joint state of

Yugoslavia and instead become the capital of the enemy state, Serbia. M was the only actress from Zagreb performing at the festival, in a production of Corneille's *L'Illusion Comique*. She knew she was the only one, but nevertheless believed that art could remain unscathed, that even in war art could preserve its freedom. In the festival bulletin she wrote that she had decided to appear at the festival in order not to lose faith in the possibility of us all working together and that in this way she was saving herself, at least temporarily, from utter despair. 'Not to play in this performance would mean signing one's own capitulation,' she said then, near the end of September 1991. The war had already been raging for several months, Osijek was being bombarded every day, the battle was on for Vukovar, the Federal Army was attacking Dubrovnik. The Zagreb–Belgrade highway was closed to traffic, the trains that used to connect the two cities by a four-hour journey were no longer running: this railway had continued to operate smoothly and regularly throughout World War II but since the summer of 1991 nobody has travelled on it. The mail service was still functioning, one could send letters, but by the autumn it was already impossible to make a phone call from one city to the other. For the last five years M had lived in both cities; she was an actress in the Croatian National Theatre in Zagreb but as her husband was working in Belgrade, she used to spend part of the time there, occasionally doing some work in a TV series or a theatre production. It was possible – complicated and sometimes exhausting – but possible nevertheless. She travelled even when the war had already started, as if trying deliberately to maintain at least some ties between the two cities to each of which half of her life belonged.

The newspapers in Croatia published her statement when

something tough and cold was already hardening in people. Attacked and driven into basements, they started to bite, to snap, especially at those who did not share their misery. Even before this, suspicions of treason had been poisoning the city like the plague, and in times of greatest danger, when the air-raid sirens howled eighteen times a day, anyone's absence was seen as cowardly at best, treachery at worst. Fear abolished the right to individual choice and what little tolerance exists in a big city, even at war, simply disappeared, evaporated into thin air. They were out to get her. The first to attack her was a woman journalist who wrote that M was parading her naked breasts on a Belgrade stage while people were being killed in Croatia. A genuine mud-raking campaign against her ensued, in the press, on television, through the grapevine. Perhaps the worst was the accusation that she was a collaborator, a Mephisto, a Gustaf Grundgens who continued to perform in the theatre after Nazi occupation. Overnight M became an enemy, publicly renounced by friends and colleagues. Had she said nothing or returned to Zagreb, things might have been different. She would not now be sitting in New York, thirty-six years old, without work, without anything, having deliberately given up her profession at the height of her career.

Her face is small, pointed, framed by long hair. Nothing except her face and hands is visible, the rest of her is hidden in a large black sweater and trousers. While she speaks, her light eyes look straight into you and her soft husky voice curls around you. In this prosperous New York apartment on the Upper East Side well isolated from street noise, where none of us belongs, M seems nervous and insecure. She sits straight-backed on the edge of an armchair, never relaxing. She has been here for two weeks now and every couple of days she moves into another apartment belonging to another friend, another acquaintance, another friend of a friend . . . She and G, her husband, came here straight from Belgrade, they did not even stop in Zagreb to pick up their winter clothes; some friends brought their suitcases and documents to Vienna and so they left, as if it were possible to get rid of the burden of their Zagreb past. She tells me she was afraid for her life and that while she was still in Belgrade she hardly ventured out in the street: it all began with the horror that had set in deep within her, which has not left her since. Now it is the middle of December and M asks me where she could buy a reasonable winter coat. I give her the names of some stores in the Village, but I cannot quite accept the fact that she and I are sitting together in New York and not in Zagreb.

I do not know what exactly took place between the publication of her statement and her departure for the States. She tells me about the letters, anonymous phone calls, insults. She speaks in short, agitated sentences, halts, speaks again. Obviously it was the phone calls that made her decide. The people who called her on the phone did not 'merely' threaten: they called her a 'Chetnik whore', they graphically, to a detail, described how they would torture her to death, which parts of the body they would cut off. She says she could feel herself die while she listened to the messages, and she heard only a small number – G would not allow her to hear the rest. Her answering machine was full. She was given a dismissal notice from the Croatian National Theatre, signed by the director, an actor who is a war orphan, a Serb from Mount Kozara whose whole family is said to have been slaughtered by the Ustashas in the last war. At first M could not believe it. Then she simply could not stay silent. She wrote 'A Letter to the Citizens of

Zagreb' and left. Now she says it is for good; I am not sure I quite believe her, because to leave the country forever is like a death sentence, it's as if part of you has been amputated.

I hereby wish to thank my co-citizens who have joined so unreservedly in this small, marginal and apparently not particularly significant campaign against me. Although marginal, it will change and mark my whole life. Which is, of course, totally irrelevant in the context of the death, destruction, devastation and atrocity crimes that daily accompanies our lives,

wrote M in her open letter, her defence and accusation at once, a letter which marked the beginning of her journey into exile.

Listening to my answering machine, to the incredible quantities of indescribably repulsive messages from my co-citizens, I longed to hear at least one message from a friend. Or not even a friend, a mere acquaintance, a colleague. But there was none. Not a single familiar voice, not a single friend. Nevertheless, I am grateful to them, to those noble patriots who kindly promise me a 'massacre the Serbian way' and to those colleagues, friends and acquaintances who by remaining silent are letting me know that I cannot count on them any more. I am grateful also to all my colleagues in the theatre with whom I played Držić, Molière, Turgenev and Shaw, I am grateful to them for their silence, I am grateful to them for not even trying to understand, let alone attempting to vindicate, my statement concerning my appearance at Bitef, the statement in which I tried to explain that taking part in that production at that moment was for me a defence of our profession which must not and cannot put itself in the service of any political or national ideas, which must not and cannot be bound by political or national boundaries because it is simply against its nature which must, even at the worst of times, establish bridges and ties . . . I cannot accept war as the only solution, I cannot make myself hate, I cannot believe that weapons, killing, revenge, hatred, an accumulation of evil could ever solve anything. Each individual who personally accepts the war is in fact an accessory to the crime; must he not then take a part of the blame for the war, a part of the responsibility?'

It was a Monday afternoon early in November, when *Danas*, the weekly that published her letter on two pages, came out. Dull winter rain was falling. Still standing in the street, I opened the paper and began to read and as I read I felt the weight of these words as if someone was just passing sentence on me. I remember reading her words, I remember the long silence which surrounded me in the middle of the city and the muted plop of raindrops falling on the paper.

It is terribly sad when one is forced to justification without having done anything wrong. There is nothing but despair, nausea and horror. I no longer have anything to make up my mind about. Others have decided for me. They have decided I must shut up, give up; they have abolished my right to do my job the way I feel it should be done, they have abolished my right to come home to my own city, they have abolished my right to return to my theatre and play in productions there . . . Can the horror of war justify each little piece of malice towards your fellow man? Can the wrong done to a friend or a colleague in the name of a great national idea be ignored? Can you, in the name of compassion with the suffering of an entire people, remain indifferent to the suffering of an individual (who also happens to be a part of this people)? These are the questions I ask my friends in

Zagreb who are now silent while at the same time they condemn Belgrade for its silence. How many petty treacheries, how many pathetic little dirty tricks must one do to remain 'clean in the eyes of the nation'?

For days that letter was the talk of the town, nobody spoke of anything else, people excitedly rolled little mudballs over their tongues: the performance was more important to her than protesting against the aggression being shown to Croatia; she may be a professional but she is no human being; how could she, we're at war, after all. Those in the know explained that her mother was Jewish and her husband Serbian: this suddenly became the key to her case, because if it wasn't for him – who had obviously made her do it – all this wouldn't have happened, M was always our little girl, our favourite, our friend, our mistress. Others said she should have returned to Zagreb, nothing would have happened to her. She has blown the whole thing out of proportion, of course, but then she has always been hysterical, hasn't she? Her colleagues were the loudest, as if by attacking her they could confirm their own political rectitude. It was not so much her defence, her protest against art being reduced to mere propaganda during the war, that aroused their ire. That did not really matter, she herself did not really matter except insofar as she articulated a moral position, a position of non-compliance and individual choice. In fact, now it was those who saw her as a Mephisto whom M was accusing of condoning the war, of being accomplices, as it were. She did not doubt that a different option was possible. Claiming they could have opted for art, M turned from the accused into the accuser and therefore had to be dealt with mercilessly. Talking about her, people actually spoke of their own moral position, of their own reasons for war. An avalanche of emotions suddenly descended upon this one person: the burden of conscience of an entire city lay on her shoulders.

'*I am sorry, my system of values is different,*' she wrote at a time when it was already out of the question to write, to say – even to think – such things because any difference, individual, political, artistic or of any other kind had already been suspended.

For me there have always existed, and always will exist, only human beings, individual people, and those human beings (God, how few of them there are) will always be excepted from generalizations of any kind, regardless of events, however catastrophic. I, unfortunately, shall never be able to 'hate the Serbs', nor even understand what that really means. I shall always, perhaps until the moment the kind threats on the phone are finally carried out, hold my hand out to an anonymous person on the 'other side', a person who is as desperate and lost as I am, who is as sad, bewildered and frightened. There are such people in this city where I write my letter. Nothing can provide an excuse any more, everything that does not directly serve the great objective has been trampled upon and appears despicable, and with it what love, what marriage, what friendship, what theatre performances! I reject, I will not accept such a crippling of myself and my own life. I played those last performances in Belgrade for those anguished people who were not 'Serbs' but human beings, human beings like me, human beings who recoil before this horrible Grand Guignol farce of bloodshed and murder. It is to those people, both here and there that I am addressing this now. Perhaps someone will hear me.

It must have been night when she sat down to write that letter. She wrote it in one go, she could not sleep. Outside they were washing the street, the slush of water and human voices rose to the window and then fell back without quite reaching her. The heating in her apartment was already turned off. G slept: he threw himself across the bed and fell asleep in his clothes as if dead tired. She could not sleep, could not shake off the feverish anxiety that had been gnawing at her for days. Then she sat at the kitchen table and wrote the letter. She read it. Like a testament, she thought, while the grey fingers of the dawn crept in through the window.

Why must everything be the same, so frighteningly uniform, levelled, standardized? Haven't we had enough of that? I know this is the time of uniforms and they are all the same, but I am no soldier and cannot be one. I haven't got it in me to be a soldier. Regardless of whether we are going to live in one, five or fifty states, let us not forget about the people, each of them individuals, no matter on which side of our wall they happen to be. We were born here by accident, we are this or that by accident, so there must be more than that, mustn't there? I am addressing this letter to emptiness, to darkness.

I carry her letter around with me as my own burden, as an inner picture of the war, as a way of explaining to others what is happening to us and our friendships in the war: how the war devours us from the inside, eating away like acid, how it wrecks our lives, how it spawns evil within us, and how we tear the living flesh of those friends who do not feel the same as we do. It is not enough that death is everywhere around us. In the war death becomes a simple, acceptable fact. But life turns to hell.

I watch her sitting on the edge of the chair, tense as if still expecting nothing but blows. She does not say much, she has said it all in the letter and now she can speak no more. She can only repeat herself. When I mention Zagreb, her cheeks burn red, she appears to be on the verge of tears. She says she does not know what she will do – what *can* a foreign actress do in someone else's city? I'd rather wash dishes, she says. Her choice, her life-changing decision is condensed into a single word: *rather*. For a while we go on sitting in a friend's apartment in a foreign city and talking about the war. We talk about how the war cannot be escaped by leaving for New York, the war is here, too. The very fact that she has left, that she has changed her life, is also the war. The war has become the pivotal point in our lives and it determines everything else. Besides, an escape also defines you, labels, determines and cripples you. I watch her lovely face aware that this is no longer a face from the movies. But I cannot see the most important things, eyes cannot reach so deep. The loneliness and the desolation of a woman who has lost her profession and her homeland can only be guessed at.

I do not tell her that the Balkan Cinema in Zagreb where she last saw all her friends has changed its name. It is now called the Europa Cinema – the name symbolically conveys the whole meaning of this war.

NEW YORK
DECEMBER 1991

85

13

IF I HAD A SON

A young boy is sitting across from me in a deep red plush armchair and drinking Coke. Although it is only eleven in the morning, on the first floor of the City Café in Zagreb a pianist in a black tuxedo is softly playing an evergreen tune. The arched windows look out on the sunlit façades around the square. It is early spring when the air is still cool and moist and there is a smell of snow. The boy gazes through the window for a while, then at the piano player and finally looks straight at me. This is not for me, I don't belong here, he says. Calmly, as if stating a simple, perfectly obvious fact. For a brief moment I am puzzled. He is wearing Levi's and a denim jacket, his hair falls over his forehead in spiky strands, he has two silver earrings in his ears – in fact, he looks like any other boy of his age who has nothing else to do but hang out in a café in the morning and play football in the afternoon. But it is not his appearance that stands as a barrier between him and the world around him – the soft hum of voices, the laughter of the waitress in the café where all the sounds from the outside are muffled – it is something else. Ivan came here from the war, from Vukovar. His father was taken prisoner (at least he hopes so, that would mean he is still alive), his house was burned down and his mother and five younger brothers and sisters are refugees. And I am a journalist puzzled by his calm, almost light voice, his calm hands on the table, his composure and, most of all, his age.

Rather than looking forward to our next meeting, I have been anxious about it. I met him two days ago. When the door of the apartment opened, I found myself in a hallway, face to face with a young boy no taller than me. His lean, narrow face still had no need for shaving. 'Is your brother at home?' I asked; I knew that the eldest brother was nineteen. One of the commanders of the Vukovar defence had told me that he and his brother had been among the twenty-six resistance fighters who were the last to retreat from Vukovar on the night of 18/19 November when the city fell. After that the Yugoslav army closed the city for twenty-four hours. They say that thousands of people simply disappeared during that time. The boys walked for three days and three nights in the rain through the enemy positions, through the cornfields, through mud, across the river, for forty-six kilometres to Vinkovci. Of some 160, most of them boys of the same age, these twenty-six were all that remained after five months of fighting. They also told me that the Croatian army soldiers applauded them when finally one morning they entered the city of Vinkovci. It was still raining. All the boys, these warriors coming into the city all caked with mud, were crying, all of them . . .

The boy in a grey Diesel sweatshirt who opened the door for me shrugged his shoulders and, pushing his chewing gum into the corner of his mouth, said, I'm the eldest. I must have made such a face the boy began to laugh. I know, I look fifteen, he said, while we went into the room in which there was nothing but a long table and a dozen chairs. Instead of a rug, a blanket was spread on the floor. This apartment had been given to them by the Croatian army headquarters; it used to belong to a Federal Army officer who moved out – in fact, fled from Croatia. The apartment had two bedrooms for the eight of them, nine, if the father returns. Ivan sat down, placed his hands on the table and looked at me in expectation.

I knew he was waiting for me to ask him questions, but I was at a loss for words. I didn't know what to ask him, caught by surprise. His face was so unbearably young that it undid me in a way. This is a story that cannot be written, I thought, not the story of this child who has lost his friends, his house, his father, even the war itself. Watching him across the table, in that empty room, perhaps for the first time I began to doubt the power of words; words, I felt, are nothing but a fragile shell, a thin wrapping which cannot protect us from reality, the sound of a stone falling into a well. Up to then I had never questioned writing, even in a time of war. It seemed to have purpose, justification, there was a way to write about war and about death. But now there was something else besides words, a silence in which you could listen to another human being.

He could be my son, I thought and could not stop thinking of it while I watched him make coffee, bring cups and rummage in the kitchen cupboard for biscuits. His hair was still wet from his morning shower, he must have got up just before I came, I thought, while he told me how his father had disappeared and for the last three months they had had no news of him as his name was not on any of the prisoner-of-war lists, about his fifteen-year-old friend who was a prisoner in a Serbian camp for a month and the beatings he got there, but he never stopped playing tricks on Federal Army officers, like pouring water into their boots. He laughed and I laughed with him, I laughed at his

88

laughter, the joy that suddenly burst from him. He told me that they heard about their house recently from their neighbours. They had seen the house being robbed (two colour TV sets, video recorder, his hi-fi set, the new, not yet completely paid-for furniture, the freezer, the fridge, carpets), they took everything, Ivan was saying, as if ticking off items from a list in his hand and then they burned it down. That's the way they do it, he explained, they load everything on to trucks and then they set the house on fire. But the house doesn't matter, he said, as if trying to cheer me up, a house can easily be built anew. He wasn't quite sure how to continue his story, I still did not ask him anything. The more talkative and open he became, the more I withdrew. I felt guilty. Not because the war did not scar me as much as it did him, one quickly learns that in war there is no justice and no equality, but because of the war itself, because this kid was forced to talk about war, he could speak of nothing else but the war, it was his life now. On the other hand, was this not precisely what I wanted, an authentic story, the smell and the taste of war? Was this not why I was sitting opposite him? In his voice I seemed to sense a slight detachment; his tone, it seemed to me, was the tone of a man making an anecdote of the war for my benefit because I could not begin to understand war on his level. It was as if he was far away and all I heard was merely a faint echo of his voice. By telling me things he thought I wanted to hear he may have been defending himself from me, from my intrusive tape recorder, from my presence. It was that tone which cast me back into the role of reporter, as if telling me, this is what you wanted, isn't it, I know perfectly well that this is what you wanted to hear. No, but no, I screamed inwardly not daring to say it out loud, not any more, not now when I've met you. I don't want to hear that story. I want us to talk about girls, school, music – just not about war, anything else but war. Trying in a way to defend myself from him, I simply refused to grasp the fact that the boy sitting here was not merely an ordinary high-school graduate who could be my son. I was afraid of his words, I was afraid of hearing what it was like to be growing up in Vukovar during those five months, in the worst place in the whole world. Tell me, what would you like best now, I asked him. That was the only thing I could utter, as if I really wanted him to stop talking, stop returning to where I did not want to follow. This was not a question he expected, I could see that he had to think about it. I'd like to walk by the river and then go to a disco. I'd like everything to be as it used to be, he said and looked at me.

He could be my son, he is four years younger than my daughter, I thought, again disturbed by his youth, and looked down at my hands, at the floor. I should not have thought of that because from the moment this thought crossed my mind again I could no longer listen to him and I could no longer speak. The words jammed in my throat, I felt I was going to suffocate. Quickly, I stood up and said good-bye. Ivan walked me to the door. We arranged another meeting in two days' time. Two days, I thought, that would give me time enough to muster the strength to face him again. After all, he is not really my son, the worst part of the war is over and Ivan is alive.

And now, in the café, I sit and watch him and it seems even worse. His presence makes me feel ill, like a kind of flu. Why did we meet again anyway? Because he was so kind? Because I insisted? But I no longer insist, it doesn't really matter any more, I have already given up on this story, this assignment. I'm trying hard to keep my cool, but I'm nervous nevertheless. He was born in 1972, I think, watching him light a cigarette. He must have started smoking only recently, in the war, yes, that must be it. There are no tell-tale yellow stains on his fingers. I could almost laugh. If this was someone else, I would tell him, you fool, quit smoking, smoking's bad for you . . . I know how the generation born in 1972 grew up, reared on Humana instant milk formula and Fructal baby food. Already there were disposable nappies and baby clothes boutiques, collapsible baby carriages from Germany and dummies from Italy. Later came battery-operated cars – that was a generation that already had too many toys – and colour TV, pinball machines, video games, walkmans, Jeans, Sneakers, Rock concerts, Madonna, MTV. It was like that in Vukovar, too. In this imitation of a Viennese Sezession café, his life unfolds before my eyes in a perfectly logical sequence that I can follow year by year as if watching my own family video. Until six or seven months ago, because that's where the movie ends. Here the thread that used to connect our lives unravels and splits.

While I watch him light his cigarette with a resolute gesture, slightly frowning as if trying to look older, I again feel horror pierce me like a cold blade: really, what if this were my own son? What would I tell him – not today at this table when the war is almost behind us, but in the early summer of 1991 in Vukovar? What would I have done, if one day he came to me and simply said, 'Mama, I'm going'? Of course, I wouldn't ask where he was going, that would have been clear by then, it could mean only one thing, going to fight in the war. I wouldn't even be surprised, perhaps I would have expected it. With fear, with anguish, but I'd be expecting it. Kids even younger than him are fighting, the kids from our street, the same generation. Some of them are already dead. But I would nevertheless tell him not to go, because this is not his war. This war began when you or I were not even born yet, what on earth makes it our war? Forget it, I'd say, no idea is worth dying for. But it's not an idea that this is all about, he'd say, I don't give a damn about ideas, about the state, about independence or democracy. They're killing my friends, they're killing them like dogs in the street and then dogs eat them because we can't get to them to bury them. How can I sit here and pretend that none of this is my business? I understand, but I didn't bring you into this world to kill or to be killed. Why do you keep talking about death? he'd ask reproachfully, as if it were stupid to speak about death, it couldn't happen to him, it happens to others. Or as if he were afraid that words had the power to make death happen. You're right, I'd say, suddenly scared of my own words, but you can't do that to me, you mustn't. Go away, somewhere, anywhere, the others are leaving, too. You can't leave here, there's no place to go, he'd say and I would know that I had already lost the battle. You're not responsible for what's happening; if anyone is to blame, then it's my generation – we saw what was going on but did nothing to prevent it. It's a war of politics where nobody cares about casualties, a war started at the very top. Everyone except the politicians is a loser. Mama, listen to me, he'd say – again this word, 'mama', which now hurts more bitterly than ever before – I know this is chaos and insanity, but I'm not going to run away. I must stay here and fight, I must defend myself and you. Defend, do you get it, it's defence and nothing else. The Serbs are kicking us out of our own homes. Does anyone have the right to do that? I don't care what was happening before I was born, believe me, I don't care at all. But this now *is* my business and my future is at stake here. If I leave now, I'll never be able to come back. That means I'll be accepting defeat lying down, and I can't do that.

The only defeat is your death, I'd say, numb with fear and powerless to stop him. Then we'd both fall silent. I would, of course, cry. He'd stand there for a while looking at me, I'd think he was hesitating, but at that moment he'd turn around and leave. Although I am not religious, I know that I would spend the rest of my time frantically trying to strike a bargain with God: God, if you exist, take me and spare him, God don't let anything happen to him and ask what you will of me in return, God let them kill me before him, God, God, God . . .

Ivan is talking and I am listening and thinking of his mother. He says that at one point she heard that both he and his younger brother had been killed and she bought black clothes for mourning with her last penny. When they called to tell her they were alive, she could not believe it until she saw them with her own eyes. She did not even recognize their voices; for her they were already dead. Then he talks about his room. It is high up in the attic, he laid and varnished the floorboards himself, he painted the walls. When he finally moved in, the room smelled of turpentine, linseed oil, varnish and wall paint for a long time. I ask him what colour he painted the walls. I painted the walls blue, the room was blue and all mine, mine only. Do you like blue? he asks me, as if this is important because it will tell him something about me. I describe the blue of the window shutters on a house in Istria, the turquoise patches on a façade that has peeled off long ago but the colour still shines through. And the blue paint used for boats and fences; he knows about these things, he's keen on them and for an instant it seems that our two pictures of the world, his and mine, mesh and engage in a single point of blueness. But then suddenly, as if interrupting something before it goes too far, Ivan says: blue is for me the colour of war. Only then do I realize that he has been talking about the house and his room in the past tense. He has been describing a picture of a room that exists only in his memory, like that special shade of blue on its walls that has not paled only in his mind's eye. And while he is talking, below his tender boyish face there emerges the face of a grown-up man for whom neither his own nor anyone else's life can have the same meaning as before. I watch him grow old before my eyes and he knows it, but that is his true face, the face of the war.

I feel now that we have both crossed the threshold of nausea. I don't have to ask him anything else, but I may, I have his silent permission. Now he is talking about the first time he was sick and how he killed a man. What corpses look like and finally, how he cried. He talks just as my son might talk, if I had a son, if he'd gone to war and if he'd stayed alive.

ZAGREB
MARCH 1992

94

14

WHAT IVAN SAID

Why did you volunteer for the Croatian Guards?
– I don't know, something in me made me do it . . .
– Because others were volunteering, too?
– It's not that so much . . . there were only a few of us at the beginning. But something drove me to it. I kept thinking I must join up, I must.
– How did you explain this to your mother?
– It was really bad for her, she thought everybody who went to fight would be killed.
– Was there fighting going on in Vukovar by then?
– Yes, my fifth day in I was already sent to mop up.
– What does that mean, 'to mop up'?
– It means you get the Chetniks and take the weapons they have stashed away.
– How did you know who had hidden weapons?
– Well, some of their own people told us, those who were scared of us, because they heard we were going to butcher them.
– And what does 'mopping up' look like?
– We came to these houses, but they already knew we were

coming. When we jumped off the truck, snipers started shooting at us. We took shelter in some houses nearby and started to shoot back, and a group of us managed to sneak up from behind, from the back.

– Who was in those houses they shot at you from, who are the Chetniks?

– The Serbs who lived there and the imported ones, the ones sent from Serbia. The reservists.

– Was this your first action?

– Yes, it was in the middle of July 1991.

– What was your job?

– I had to cover the others because the commander wouldn't let me fight, I was the youngest. What you do is you take a position and keep a look-out.

– You had a gun? You knew how to use it?

– An automatic. I learned to shoot way back, in April. The older guys taught me.

– Where did they get the weapons from?

– Bought them.

– So people had already been preparing for war?

– Yes, for quite some time. In Vukovar the Croats were getting armed. The Serbs already had weapons, they would walk around and boast about it.

– And how did you feel going into your first action?

– Can't say I was totally cool about it.

– Fear?

– It's not exactly fear, it's like . . . you're afraid you're going to get killed. That's all you can think about.

– What kind of feeling is it, then, if you say it's not fear, how do you tell it apart from fear?

– I think fear's got more to do with panic, and this is . . . like, you're afraid of dying, why you, what if now . . . and you can't get it out of your head . . .

– Let's go back to your first action.

– There was only one house with Chetniks in it, the rest of them ran away into the wood across the Vuka river, into Bršadin. There were perhaps two or three of them in that house and we wanted to make them surrender. We went into the house but couldn't find them. Then we saw this narrow door leading to the basement, one of our guys was about to open the door when a bullet pierced his hand, it came from down below. You couldn't get down there, the staircase was too narrow. We asked them to come out, we told them nothing would happen to them, they'd be tried in court. And they kept yelling from below, you're Ustashas, you'll slaughter us. Then another of our guys tried to get down there and got shot in the shoulder. Then his friend got really mad, went behind the house, opened a small basement window and threw a bomb inside. And then, when we went to the basement, that's the first time I saw it . . .

– What did you see?

– People blown up and torn to pieces. One or two men, it couldn't have been more than that. The basement was small, you couldn't really tell how many of them were there. They were mincemeat, all that was left of them was blood stains on the wall. Everything was spattered with blood. I went out. I didn't really care because I'd had no part in it, it wasn't me that . . .

– But when you see that . . .

– But it's not . . . the feeling isn't the same.

– Later you got used to seeing things like that?

– I remember one Saturday, it was raining and we were

resting, like. And there was this air raid. They mostly machined-gunned from the planes, seven of our guys were wounded. That day was the worst for me. I saw a shell fall on a car and it burst into flames. There were people inside that car.

— Were they civilians?

— Civilians. A neighbour of mine was driving, he used to live a hundred yards from my house. His brother was sitting in the back. The fire had already caught him and he was all scorched, we tried to pry the doors open but he was already dead. For the first time in my life I saw skin melt off a man, that was . . . everything is in flames, the car is burning, the man is sitting inside with his eyes wide open, and there's nothing anyone can do. His head just sinks lower and his face melts. A bullet wounds you or kills you, but this, it's like the movies, like setting a wax doll on fire. The flesh on his arms burned off to the bones.

— They say that corpses were lying in the streets of Vukovar.

— I first saw a heap of corpses when someone came and said people couldn't sleep because of the stench of dead bodies in the cornfield. Because they left their dead behind, even the wounded. They never came back to pick them up.

— Who came to tell you about the corpses?

— The guys who held the position in the houses at the edge of the city, near the cornfields. It was summer and very hot, they said it stank like hell. Dogs were coming, there was a danger of diseases spreading. Something had to be done, the place had to be cleaned up. We loaded a truck full of corpses.

— You also helped to load the corpses on to the truck?

— No, I couldn't do it, I just stood by. I couldn't really take it. As soon as I got there, I began to vomit. People, dead people, rotting, decaying, flies coming out of their mouths. I just collected weapons.

– Do you know who those dead people were?

– Their men. All older guys, reservists and volunteers with beards. Only two of them were from Borovo, that's a town nearby, they joined the Chetniks. We took their IDs from their pockets and piled them all together in a big heap; they were all from Serbia, from Pazova, Niš, mostly from Šid. We drove the truck to the bank of the River Danube, there was this large hole and we buried them in it. But after one truck-load the hole was full. There was no place to bury them any more, so we made a pile of bodies near the water tower and burned them. The money we burned, too, nobody was allowed to touch their money. The commander's orders. We just kept the IDs.

– Did you get used to the whole thing?

– I did, you turn into a machine. You simply work like a machine. You think like a man and act like a robot. You've got to. Because if you have any feelings left . . . there . . . in the war . . .

– How do you know you've turned into a machine?

– You just know it, you think in a different way. See, we caught one of theirs, from Šid. He was a reservist, thirty years old, but very extreme, you could tell straight away. He had a membership card of the Chetniks' party and a photo of Šešelj, the Chetnik leader. We gave him some hope, we told him it's going to be all right, we'd trade him for one of our own although the chances for trading prisoners were slim, they killed our guys on the spot. But one of our fighters was missing. We called their barracks, we thought that maybe we could work out an exchange of prisoners. The whole conversation took place in front of this Chetnik, he could hear everything. From the barracks they said: those men of ours that you've captured don't deserve to live if they've allowed themselves to fall into the hands of the Ustashas. When we capture yours, you know what we do to them. And they hung up? And this reservist, he started to laugh, he was proud of it . . .

– Proud? Of what?

– Of what this man in the barracks said, that we know what they do to our guys. Like he was nuts, like he didn't cotton on to the fact that he was our prisoner. The guys jumped on him, started to hit him. All those days while we held him prisoner he kept cursing us and our Ustasha mothers. We gave him food, nobody beat him, nothing. You came up to him and he spat at you. Then, of course, one of our guys flipped out, came to the commander and said, you take me to court, but I'm going to kill this man. The commander forbade it, but . . . we went down to the basement, this guy untied him. The Danube river was two hundred yards from us. He made him go into the water and then he killed him.

– Although the commander forbade it?

– But, you see, the war had already started. In war you listen to your commander but the commander allows you to do what you think is best for you. Because he gives orders, but it's you who's going to get killed.

– Have you seen many things like that happening?

– I never saw our guys butcher anybody or use a knife on a reservist. I did see something else . . . a man being beaten to death.

– A reservist?

– No, he was a local Serb who turned Chetnik, he was twenty-five. It was a hundred per cent certain that he had murdered some of our people. He himself admitted to two of our fighters that he'd killed their parents – the father and mother of one and the father of the other. He told them that openly because they used to be friends before.

– Did he tell them why he did it?

– He just said, you're Ustashas, this is Serbia. One Serb escaped from their barracks and confirmed all that had been said about his slaughtering people. When we caught him, the boys whose parents he had murdered came, two brothers, one twenty-eight and the other twenty-three. This man butchered both their father and mother. And the third guy, he's twenty-three and his brother was killed. One day this man cut the throat of his father, and on the next day his brother was killed in the battle . . . And he says, Is it true what they're saying, that you killed my father? And the man says, Yeah, it's true, I killed your father. And this guy says, Why? The man says, Because you're Ustasha. And this guy says, And earlier, when we were pals, was I a Ustasha then? No, he says, but you went over to them. Our guys got really mad like and jumped on him. They beat him like hell, it's hard to describe. They beat him and they cried, because he used to be their friend.

– And you saw this?

– We all stood there and watched, fifty of us.

– Fifty of you just stood there and watched as the three of them beat him up?

– They beat him up one by one. Later the others went mad, too. This used to be a tight group of friends, those four guys and a couple of others. They were friends until July, and then this Serb went away and when he came back, he was a Chetnik. They had been together since they were sixteen. And when they heard he was caught after he had killed their parents . . .

– What did they beat him with? Did they kick him with their feet?

– They beat him with everything, sticks, everything . . . And

I couldn't condemn them for what they did. If someone told me he had murdered my parents, I'd kill him right away. I didn't feel sorry for him, not a bit, though I knew him, too. I had no feelings towards him, but I didn't want to beat him. I just stood there, didn't get involved, because they were beating him. And suddenly this other guy grabbed him by the chin and twisted his head. He just grabbed him and wrenched, like this . . . They beat him until he died. Then they threw him into the Danube.

    – Did any of your commanders know about that?

    – They did . . .

    – But they couldn't do anything?

    – There's not much anyone can do. When someone tells you he has murdered your Mum and Dad. Even if the highest-ranking commanding officer came and told you you mustn't kill this man, it wouldn't work. It's revenge.

    – And this was the worst thing that happened?

    – The worst was when I killed a man for the first time.

    – You mean, from close up?

    – Yes. There were three of us, my brother, myself and a friend of ours. We went out to meet them. We hid in a house some fifty yards from their barracks and we saw them coming, three of them, carrying backpacks.

    – What were they?

    – Reservists.

    – How can you tell who are reservists?

    – You can tell them right away, they have beards, they're shabby, they stink of liquor, they really stink, that's no lie. They went around robbing people's houses. We let them approach to about five yards away, they were coming towards us but didn't see us.

– To five yards precisely?

– Yes, but they couldn't see us because the sun was in their eyes and we were in the basement. When they came close, this friend of mine, who was on the ground floor, came out of the house and told them to drop their weapons. We wanted to take them prisoner. Then they pointed their machine-guns at us and we just blew them away. We came up to them to take their weapons, we took their backpacks, too, because we thought they might be carrying bombs, but we saw it was phones so we left them there.

– Phones?

– Phones! And all sorts of things, they'd even steal clothes. I couldn't sleep all night. I had done it before . . . from afar. I saw the man fall when I shot him. But the feeling's not the same, not even remotely. You're standing right before him, he begins to lift his gun and you just . . . It's like a machine, there's no feeling to it, no thinking. Either he's going to get you or you're going to get him. And then what was really terrible, I took the gun from the man I had killed and I saw that it wasn't even loaded! He did aim at me but he couldn't really shoot: the gun wasn't cocked and wasn't loaded. He raised his gun mechanically while he knew all the time he couldn't shoot. I was younger, he thought I would get scared and throw down my gun. But when I saw him aim at me, I just shot him, just like that and . . . it was over.

– Do you still remember what the man looked like, his face?

– Yes . . .

– You remember the faces?

– Yes, you do . . . The next day we were keeping watch in a house near the tank route and we saw two soldiers coming. My friend took the sniper's rifle, he wanted to kill them without making too much noise so we wouldn't be noticed. But then he lowered the gun, he said these soldiers were young army draftees, not reservists. They were about fifty yards from us. They had white belts, they were their military police. When they got to about ten yards from us, we yelled at them to stop and drop their weapons, but they began firing at us. In fact, they fired at the house, they didn't see us. One of them almost shot my brother, then my brother returned fire and shot him. The other one threw himself on the ground, we could only see his arm with the gun. My brother and another friend sneaked up to him with grenades, came to within two or three yards of him and when they saw he was wounded, he cried for help. They told him to give himself up and nothing would happen to him. Or they'd throw a grenade. When he gave himself up, we saw he was really just a kid.

– So he was a draftee and not a reservist?

– Yeah, a draftee from Niš. We felt sorry for him, he was born in 1972, like me . . .

– What happened to him then?

– We took him to the hospital, they bandaged him there and he was sent to Zagreb with the first convoy out of Vukovar. He could choose, he could go to Belgrade, if he wanted to. We talked to him, we took some juice to him because there was no juice in the hospital and finally we made friends with him. His name was Srdjan. He told us to bring him the red star from his cap and he'd eat it before our eyes! He had only now realized that they'd been made to go to war against Croatia and he wasn't guilty, he said, because he didn't volunteer, he was drafted. Within fifteen days only two out of his entire group of thirty-six had survived. The rest were killed. And all of them were born in 1972 or 1973, just like us . . .

– Did you look for him in Zagreb?

– I did, I thought he might be at the Rehabilitation Centre, but I didn't find him. I only found a friend of our commander who had lost both legs.

– How did this happen?

– It was the day of the big battle on Trpinjska cesta. We couldn't find our commander and the other fighters told us to look for him in the hospital. We asked the doctor where our commander was but the doctor said, I'm not going to tell you anything, go down to the basement and see for yourself. The commander was lying there and beside him was his brother, stroking his head. When we came closer, we saw that the commander's left leg was blown in half, the lower half was missing, while his right leg was scorched completely and so was his right hand. We stayed with him for two hours without saying a single word, we just wept. He's twenty-two. I think that's when I felt worst.

– Why then?

– He was our commander not because someone appointed him but because we picked him to be our commander. He was a brave man, tall, six feet eight perhaps, and strong. He wasn't afraid of anything. We looked up to him, all of us. And when I saw him lying there, without legs, crippled and totally helpless . . . I felt terrible.

– Did it perhaps occur to you to quit at that moment?

– No, it didn't, once you're inside you can't get out, you can't quit.

ZAGREB
MARCH 1992

15

AND THE PRESIDENT IS DRINKING
COFFEE ON JELAČIĆ SQUARE

It was on Saturday 22 February at five minutes to one in the afternoon that I saw the new Croatian President Franjo Tudjman for the first time. I saw him through a huge, thick glass window of a very posh café on Duke Jelačić Square. The café was full of people squashed at French-type tables of fake marble. But I could not tell if they were mainly ordinary visitors or bodyguards, only two of whom – tall, good-looking boys – I could make out by the door and two others sitting at the table next to his. I also noticed a few old ladies looking at the President with adoration while eating their tarts and drinking espresso. The rest of the people in the café generally seemed to be pretending not to be excited, that he was nobody special or that they meet him at least twice a week in this same place – a Central European kind of custom. Dressed in a dark grey suit and a white shirt tied tightly with a dark blue tie, he sipped his coffee slowly: not Turkish coffee, I suppose, since that is what those barbarian Serbs usually drink while we Europeans drink espresso or capuccino or perhaps a 'mélange'. He looked relaxed and in a good mood, apparently amused by what a much younger man whom I recognized from TV as one of his advisers was telling him, leaning across the table to get closer to his ear. The President smiled, barely parting his lips: one more of his famous unpleasant smiles – he couldn't do much about that, I guess – which gave his face the expression of a bird, an owl perhaps. When he lifted his head with a tiny white cup in his hand to look through the window to the square I could tell from the look that he didn't really see either the window or the square behind it. His thoughts were far away, far beyond us all standing there, the kind of look that makes you feel like an extra in a Hollywood B-production, a super-spectacle about the war in the Balkans.

In front of the café window, surprisingly enough, there were not many people, only a few reporters who ran between this scene and a crowd of some several hundred people at the eastern-edge of the square, not more than thirty yards from the café. It was a protest meeting of people from Vukovar, civilians and fighters together, people who had lost their homes as their entire city of 50,000 inhabitants had been shelled to ruins in the previous months. They had called the meeting because they were not getting the kind of help from the government that had been promised, from payment to soldiers and wounded people, to apartments and financial help for relatives of the thousands of victims. The other thing that outraged them was the way a police had intimidated a man who, until three months ago, was the leader of defence of Vukovar, a war commander nicknamed Hawk, whom all the soldiers as well as the media acclaimed as a hero. Nonetheless he was arrested and when everything else failed, including a charge of treason, he had been accused of the theft of some 300,000 German marks in cash, collected by Croats living abroad in order to buy arms for Vukovar. Everyone knew that behind his arrest there was a much bigger political issue because Hawk had accused the Croatian army headquarters, the government and the President himself of deliberately withholding arms from Vukovar and of not giving permission to evacuate remaining civilians from the city before the Serbian army entered it. Hawk claimed that as a result some 4000 civilians had either been killed or disappeared. The police held him in prison for about a month where he was severely beaten and tortured, as he later told reporters. Then they let him go, but the investigation is still continuing.

I went across to join the meeting. I saw a group of people in front of TV cameras, standing under a cold drizzle. 'Even the sky shows us no mercy,' said a woman behind me. Hawk was just explaining to the surprised journalists that the police authorities had cut off power to the microphones even though they'd sought regular permission for the meeting days in advance, just as one had to do in the days of the communist regime. And in just the same way (what else could one expect when most of the key men in the police had remained to work for the new state?) they'd had their the electricity supply cut off at the last moment, permission or no permission. A tall, strong-looking man had informed the people waiting in the rain, but they decided to hold a meeting anyway. Another man, rather old and skinny, who I later heard was a famous doctor from the Vukovar underground hospital, climbed on an improvised 'stage' made of plastic boxes at the end of Jelačić Square, and started to talk to the people there, but his weak voice was carried away by the wind and the murmuring of the crowd. But the people gathered in the square didn't sound angry; from their faces they looked as if they knew something like this was to be expected after everything else that had been done, or rather not done for them by this government and this city, where the days of the week still had a proper meaning, where people could still treat the Saturday family lunch as if it were the most important thing in the world.

But what was the President doing, there in the same square, while several hundred people stood in the rain, unable to voice their disillusionment? Did he know about it or had his advisers, his secretaries, his bodyguards, his servants simply told the President that there had been some minor problems with the trams running in this rain ('You know, Mr President, how capricious these trams become in wet weather,' someone could have said to him). I went back to the café. He still sat there, and just as I arrived I saw a short woman dressed all in black with messy hair, maybe in her fifties pass the bodyguard and stop by the President. She began to talk to him in what seemed a calm tone of voice. As the President turned his head in surprise two men rose from their chairs and grabbed the woman's arms. The situation was tense, some people stood up in confusion. Some left. But the woman just stood there talking (he obviously didn't order her out) as if she didn't care what happened to her. When the bodyguard let her free she pointed several times to the mass of people whom he hadn't, or didn't want, to notice. He shook his head. To everything this woman said he simply shook his head. That was all he did: I never saw him once open his mouth and talk to her. The woman went out, her face racked with pain. People in the café sat back and continued to drink, gesticulating. The President continued to talk to a man on his left as if it had been just another unimportant interruption, a little incident that would do nothing to disturb his intention of spending a peaceful, pleasant Saturday morning in this café in the city of his great victory. After all, this kind of thing must be expected to happen when one is President but wants to go out just as an ordinary citizen. And this is what bodyguards are for, to take care of such little nuisances. But the woman didn't go away. She stood there, in front of the café, pale and beside herself, looking as if she'd faint any minute. To the small group of people who gathered around her she explained that she had gone in there as a delegate of the protest meeting to ask the President to address them. 'I didn't ask him to give us a speech, just to come and greet us, to say a couple of nice words to the citizens of the non-existent city,' she said, her voice cracking under the heavy burden of her words. 'But our President is drinking coffee on Jelačić Square while his people, his fighters, stand in the rain waiting. Waiting for what? Now we know that we are not worth even a few words any more . . .'

The crowd in front of the café was growing, but not a single hostile voice was raised. They were in a kind of stupor, a stupor of disbelief. The fact that the President couldn't even bother to acknowledge them was so painful that they could barely speak, as if such a level of arrogance was hard to imagine and now that their city had disappeared, it would be best if they disappeared too. For how many of the 1.2 million citizens of Zagreb came to the square to greet them or offered help in support of their demands? As my colleague remarked, one could single out without difficulty almost every person from Zagreb who had come – as if people from Vukovar were in some way contagious, bringing a germ of war to the city that was trying so hard to forget. 'Perhaps it would be better if we all got killed, not only ten thousand of us,' said a young boy, and I could feel that there was anger in his voice when he added, 'I'll never forget this', but more as if he were angry at himself or his other fellow-citizens for coming there at all.

I went back to the café window. Behind it, as if in a big aquarium, the President stood up. He'd decided that he had had enough of his stroll for today, enough of seeing his own people too. Smilingly he shook hands with some of the customers who were obliged to acknowledge that he was not an ordinary visitor after all. Oddly enough, from where I stood, it looked as if he were congratulating them on something. Leaving the café he turned back and waved to the waiters with his left hand – how quickly, how easily new leaders learn that imperial gesture! Meanwhile the group outside stood waiting for him, to come out and perhaps to stop for a moment. But he crossed the threshold and just passed by. He didn't look to his left, where it was obvious that something was happening, not even out of curiosity. As he passed the group there was a stiff silence. I heard one man coughing nervously. Then the tall man who had addressed the meeting at the start, to tell them that the microphones had been cut off, went after the President. Approaching him from behind, he took the President by the sleeve of his coat. The President turned around; again there was a nervous jam around the two of them. Someone pointed at another man standing next to the President whom, I recognized as the Prime Minister. So the man from Vukovar then approached the minister and started to talk to him instead. Together they went back to the group. The President stood for about five minutes watching it all from the edge of the square, waiting for his Prime Minister to return. I took a closer look: the President was tall, taller than I imagined from TV pictures. He was good-looking too, for a seventy-year-old man, dressed in a well-tailored black coat, with grey hair and a

111

straight, somewhat rigid posture that indicated an ex-soldier. There was an air about him, as he looked around, of a general surveying the battlefield with an expert's eye. Concluding that at that moment there was no battle worth fighting, he turned his back on the square and left.

The Prime Minister was left behind to argue with a group of a dozen or so. The same woman who had approached the President approached him too, perhaps repeating the whole story or asking for an explanation. All I could hear were his words in a high voice: 'But I promise you . . .' To this day I don't know what his promise was or if he kept it at all. When he too left the group they returned to the gathering on the other side of the square still waiting in the rain that was now pouring down. By now many people had left, the journalists too (not much of a story here, they thought). Hawk stood there smoking and nodding at the story about the President that the tall man was telling him: 'I knew, I told you that he was not going to do that,' he said. Again I thought how strange it was, this visible absence of anger, as if people were too tired, too devastated to bother with anger.

At that moment, as I looked at them clustered around talking to each other, the survivors of Vukovar seemed to me to have lost yet another battle in this square where the President was taking his coffee, humiliated by the fact that he didn't want to be disturbed by some protest meeting, that he didn't want to hear about Vukovar any longer. At least not now, not today, Saturday 22 February. On this day he had other, more important things on his mind. They were invisible for him, nonexistent from where he sat, from the broad historical perspective he clearly had in view: the independence of Croatia recognized by the European Community just a couple of days ago, the realization of a thousand-year-old dream of the Croatian people, diplomacy, big powers, the enemy. Who could blame him for not noticing a few hundred people in Jelačić Square?

It was at five minutes to two when the President left the square. A small incident was over, the case of Vukovar publicly closed, the war almost over, or so he thought at the time. This was the first time I saw the new Croatian President Franjo Tudjman.

ZAGREB
MARCH 1992

16

THE WOMAN WHO STOLE AN
APARTMENT

I would have never had thought that a timid, fragile girl like her was capable of stealing anything, much less a whole five bedroom apartment. Probably she didn't consider herself a thief either, which is precisely the problem. But nevertheless, this is what she tried to do.

Ana – although of course this is not her real name – is twenty-six years old and already an accomplished young journalist. She started to write while still at high school. In a way, she was forced to support herself. Once she told me that she was from a poor farming family, from a village about forty miles from Zagreb. When she came here to secondary school, her parents didn't have money to pay for her schooling in a big city, so seeing no future for herself in the place where she was born, she had to find a way to survive in Zagreb. She started to write for a youth magazine. Modest as she was, she needed only a little money and that was an ideal place to earn it and to learn a profession too. Curiously – curious, that is, only in the light of what she did later – she was interested above all in writing about social issues. It was a very unpopular subject among young reporters who preferred to hang around the city and have fun. If they had a sharp tongue, and could write with wit and humour about movies, books, the theatre or culture in general, they even stood a good chance of making a name.

This is why Ana's choice was unusual and welcomed by the editorial board of permanent 'students' in their thirties who were only waiting to grab an opportunity to start work on a 'big', real paper. On the other hand, for anyone who knew her it wasn't such a strange choice. The first thing that struck you about Ana was her seriousness. Perhaps that's why she gave an impression of being older than she was. Even if her face framed with limp blonde hair looked childish, its expression was tense and stern and her whole attitude quiet and withdrawn. If she lacked one thing, it was a sense of humour. One always had the feeling that Ana was very dutiful – towards her parents, at school (she was an excellent student), at her job. If her writing lacked style, she compensated for it with accuracy and reliability and she had a feeling for a good story as well. I remember her articles on tramps, beggars, prostitutes, public kitchens and numerous other social injustices that the communist government would have preferred to brush under the carpet. However, the overall impression was that of diligence, of the dutiful pupil.

As soon as she finished her journalistic studies at the faculty of political sciences she started to free-lance for a big political weekly and soon became a staff writer following the same kind of stories there. She was the youngest member of staff and everyone liked her. This was when I came to know her better. I even considered her something of my own 'child', someone I especially cared about. I was impressed by the fact that she, only two years older than my daughter, was working for a serious magazine. The other thing that struck me about her was that she had supported herself all through her school and university years.

One day Ana came to me crying. I'd never seen her in that state, usually she was able to control herself and to handle her problems without help. But this time she was desperate: she had to leave a rented apartment she lived in and didn't have anywhere to move to. It was the beginning of the school year in 1990 and the city was full of students searching for apartments, the worst possible time to be thrown out. By coincidence, my friend – let's call her Marta – had just moved out of her apartment to join her husband in Belgrade. Although she could have got good money renting it to a foreign businessman for example, she didn't want to let it but instead was looking for someone to stay there to take care of her valuable collection of paintings. When she asked me if I could recommend someone I told her about Ana. In my view, she was an ideal candidate, young, responsible and without money. I put them in touch and Marta was happy to entrust her apartment to her. Suddenly relieved of the need to search further and with the prospect of staying there for a couple of years at least, Ana was overjoyed.

In the following months the situation on our magazine changed considerably for the worse and Ana left for what she thought would be a better paid job in a new daily newspaper which went down after just two months of publishing. Shortly afterwards, she started to work for another new magazine, a sensational political tabloid, a particular kind of publication characteristic of all ex-communist countries after 1989. I would never have thought she would have been willing to work for such a paper, but I didn't want to blame her too much because, to tell the truth, there was not much choice.

In the meantime, war had broken out in Croatia and I spoke to her a few times on the telephone. She sounded saturated with emotion, confused and unable to analyse the new political situation, succumbing more and more to the phenomenon of total national homogenization. It was not hard for this to happen to her because, like the rest of her generation, she was not only completely depoliticized (which actually meant a refusal to discuss or understand politics, as a form of rebellion against the then apparently immutable communist regime) but also lacked the education, the intellectual means for analysis of this kind.

During that time Marta was commuting between the two cities of Belgrade, where her husband lived, and Zagreb where she was a professor at the university. When in Zagreb, she stayed in her brother's apartment. Her brother was a diplomat in one of the African countries, diplomacy happening to be a family tradition. Their late father, a well-known and highly placed party leader in post-war Yugoslavia, served first in the government and then as ambassador to many countries in the West; as a result Marta had spent half her life in Berlin, Rome, Paris, Geneva and so on. In fact, she had never lived for a long period of time either in Zagreb or anywhere else in her own country. She was more of a cosmopolitan orientation, spoke at least four languages fluently and had a lot of excellent connections abroad – a common curriculum vitae for the children of the 'red bourgeoisie'. There is no doubt that she – as opposed to Ana – was a member of Yugoslavia's communist elite and so she never suffered from any lack of apartments, foreign travel, books or the company of interesting people. After all, she herself was a philosopher and the author of a number of books, in short a respected intellectual in her own right.

When the war approached Zagreb with the air-raid alarms of mid-September 1991, she wrote about her experiences for Belgrade's leading liberal opposition paper. Describing the atmosphere of growing fear, suspicion and danger, she wrote:

> *This is such a narrowing of the human horizon as I could never have imagined before. A person is reduced to one dimension only, that of the nation; a culture is reduced to limited and hastily invented national symbols; we all become shortsighted. They have enclosed us within narrow borders we never knew existed and now we are culturally suffocating – not to mention the physical suffering of countless dead and wounded. We are all going to choke like mice. We are never going to get out of this nationalist discourse, Croatian or Serbian alike. We'll never be able to build our future on that, we'll be thrown back perpetually into the past, far back into the past.*

She goes on to describe her neighbours turning into self-appointed policemen, dirty cellars sheltering people far too ready to collaborate with the war, the way one becomes an enemy. She concludes:

> *This is not my state and my city. I wasn't born here.*

The reaction to her article was as vehement as it was unexpected. It wasn't the fact that she wrote for a magazine in what was already the enemy state of Serbia, because it was well known for taking a pro-Croatian position anyway. It was more that it was a clear sign that she'd gone 'too far' in expressing her individualism, her unwillingness to participate in what she called 'war games'. However, she had chosen perhaps the most unhappy moment of the war in Croatia: Osijek was being shelled every day, Vukovar had been surrounded and was systematically being destroyed, the blockade of Dubrovnik had just begun, many Croat villages had been burned down and a river of hundreds of thousands of refugees from the occupied territory was flooding Zagreb. Young boys, her students, were getting killed. Yet she had written of feeling imprisoned in the city, as if it were a *jail*, as if she were *displeased* with what was going on.

The letters that appeared in the press were bitter: she was accused of cynicism and lack of empathy, but most of all, for equating the victim with the executioner. In the eyes of the public, she had become a traitor, a 'fifth columnist'. This Marta couldn't understand, she couldn't understand that every occasion for public discussion, for intellectual nuances or plain differences of opinion had suddenly been poisoned, usurped, swept away by the war. Under the everyday threat of shelling (between 15 September and 4 November there were forty air-raid alarms in Zagreb, the front line was less than twenty miles away, the presidential palace in the middle of the old city was hit as well as villages on the outskirts of Zagreb) things became black and white. Moreover, she was perceived as a person who wrote from Olympian heights, as someone who had other options, who could go somewhere else if she wanted, while the majority couldn't even think of an alternative. So the message against her in the media was: *Go! Get out of this city and don't come back!*

It was hard to find a single person to defend her position even among the people who knew her. 'You agree that her apartment should be taken away from her, don't you?' I heard one of her acquaintances saying. In fact this was not the first time that her apartment had been mentioned; one of the hate-letters published in a magazine mentioned that she lived in a 'big, luxurious apartment in the very centre of the city', as if by living there she'd committed a crime in itself, or as if, having been proclaimed as 'enemy of the people', she didn't 'deserve' such an apartment at all.

Now, the story of her apartment is the story of the majority of apartments in this country: they were communal property, state owned. But because the party ruled in the name of the people, it also meant they were, in a broader sense, owned by the people – nominally, at least. In short, these apartments were rented through state-owned companies and in reality no one could take them from a person who had a certain type of contract. One's children too were entitled to the same rights. Marta, in fact, had inherited the apartment from her father. The proposal I heard from her acquaintance was thus by no means illogical: she was only talking about the typical bolshevik method of stripping her of the right to live there, similar to the method of nationalization or confiscation of property belonging to 'enemies of the state' after World War II and the communist revolution in Yugoslavia. This was the mood of the people about her 'case'.

Confronted by such a violent onslaught Marta was frightened. She finally understood that the war was not happening simply to others, but to her as well and that this was the way she was experiencing it. Words too, she learned, could become a dangerous weapon. As she had already received a six-month grant to teach in France, she left soon after for Paris.

Time passed but 'Marta's case' didn't disappear under the welter of troubles that now hit Croatia. Periodically her name would pop up here and there in articles discussing, listing or enumerating traitors, dissidents, enemies, cowards and so on. Obviously, this purge of 'internal enemies' was an aspect of the war in the city and it was related to something which no one would admit to in words – revenge. Many apartments left by such people were broken into, especially those left behind by Federal Army officers, but not only by countless refugees, but by ordinary, self-righteous individuals who saw a way to solve the problems of their own inadequate living conditions and didn't see anything wrong in usurping the apartment of an 'enemy'.

A couple of months after she left, an article by a popular woman columnist appeared discussing the matter of Marta's apartment. 'I am very concerned,' she wrote sarcastically, 'that poor Marta – so disgusted by Croatia that she had to leave for Paris – might now be permitted to buy a communal apartment from that same disgusting republic. As an ambassador's daughter, ambassador's wife and ambassador's sister, Marta was used to getting everything from Yugoslavia for free. Perhaps it would be good therefore to give her the apartment for free too, so she doesn't report us to the Helsinki Tribunal.' The columnist (who knew her personally) concluded that greedy Marta had acquired the apartment at the people's expense.

Reading this, I realized that the information about Marta's attempt to buy off the apartment from the state had come from Ana. Not only did Ana live in Marta's apartment, so she was bound to know about it, but she also worked for the newspaper in which the article had appeared. However, it was very hard to believe that Ana had any reason to give away this type of information, that she would have any reason to do it at all. I then asked around and discovered that Marta had come back from Paris during the Easter holidays to arrange to buy the apartment when the new law permitting that possibility was passed. After living in her apartment for more than a year free and because Ana and her boyfriend were now making decent money as journalists, Marta had asked them if they'd be willing to pay a rent by monthly instalments according to the new economic prices set by the government, which wouldn't cost them more than renting another apartment.

On the telephone, Ana didn't say a word. But the first thing next morning she went to the special commission of the Croatian Parliament (the official owner of the apartment) denouncing Marta for not even living in the apartment she was attempting to buy, suggesting that she should be denied the right to buy it because she was a war profiteer of a kind and that the apartment should in fact be taken from her. Perhaps Marta should be given a smaller apartment to buy, she added, not the big one she inherited from her father. As for herself, Ana didn't claim the right to the apartment directly, but she did think she and her boyfriend deserved something. I don't know if Ana mentioned the word 'reward' but this is what she meant.

Having heard what Ana had done, Marta went to a lawyer and started proceedings, first to expel Ana and her boyfriend from her apartment and second, to assert her right to buy it under the new legislation. The problem is, however, that until Ana withdraws the claim she lodged with the government Marta won't be able to buy the apartment and with an ongoing war, this could take forever. It also means that Ana could continue living in Marta's apartment (which she is doing) until the case is legally resolved. In the meantime, when Marta went to the same Parliament commission, she found that the file containing her application to buy the apartment had simply vanished, together with the rest of her documents!

In essence, Ana has tried to steal the apartment. Not for herself – and this is the point, because this is where her sense of 'justice' comes in – but so that she can give it back to the state, to 'the people'. She is doing a favour to the state by reporting on a person of communist background, and a traitor too, who doesn't deserve to have such a luxurious apartment. But this tiny, timid, diligent reporter with a special sense of justice and duty has demonstrated a sound instinct for the realities of war too; in her judgement, this has been the perfect chance literally to take the law into her own hands. Never mind the fact that the apartment was entrusted to her or that she didn't pay a rent for it. At the 'right' moment, when Ana saw that it was possible to act according to the new rules of the game, she was able to abandon any moral scruples. Indeed, when she saw the chance for a girl like herself from the provincial proletariat to get something for nothing, she didn't hesitate. Given the opportunity, aren't others – refugees, soldiers, ordinary citizens, even a neighbour in the same building – doing the same? The newspapers are full of stories of this kind, people talk about it in local bars and supermarkets, in every neighbourhood there are similar cases. And what happens to them? Nothing. So Ana must have thought, Why not me? She didn't see herself as someone who would denounce people in an attempt to profit by it, she didn't see that she was taking it upon herself to judge who should be left without an apartment and for what reason. But most important of all, Ana wouldn't have dared do what she did if Marta hadn't been proclaimed a 'traitor'. In this way, Ana saw no harm done: the people give, the people take away.

When I discussed the matter with a friend familiar with the case she said to me: 'Are you sure that Ana was wrong in doing this? When Marta's father was given the apartment it had most probably been taken from a rich Jew, a bourgeois or enemy of the people during the previous regime.' This is very likely the truth, but on the other hand Marta's mother's family house as well as several apartments were also confiscated and no doubt given to someone else in turn – namely, to someone who 'deserved' it because of their achievements during the War. If you want to correct historical mistakes and restore justice – which is not the task of the individual anyway, but of the law – the question is how far back do you go and what is the point in doing it if you allow the very same pattern to be repeated?

However, even the 'revolutionary law' of Tito's partisans was different from breaking the law, which is what Ana did. But if one asked Ana, I am afraid she would see no harm in the 'new bolshevism' or her own act. In my view she merely behaved as the dutiful, diligent child of communism. By her act she merely showed she had graduated in the revanchism of the proletariat against its class enemy: this time the communist or 'red bourgeoisie' itself. Just as she'd been taught in their school.

ZAGREB
APRIL 1992

17

A LETTER TO MY DAUGHTER

Zagreb, 7 April 1992

My dear R,

This morning I went to your empty room. Its tidiness was so strange: your usually unmade bed now covered with a blue quilt, a clean desk (with a sticker: A clean desk is a sign of a sick mind!), a chair without your T-shirts hanging from it, a carpet without at least three pairs of shoes scattered around and your two dogs Kiki and Charlie playing with a yellow rubber ball. I miss you, I miss your voice, your messages written with a lipstick on a bathroom mirror, your little notes that you leave on the table when you come in late at night and which I read with my first morning coffee.

Just today it is nine months since you left the country. Nine months is such a long time, I thought as I sat there for a moment, time for a baby to be born. What a strange thought. Or perhaps not so strange after all because you are now a grown woman and could decide to have a baby yourself. And because what was born in the past nine months was not a baby but a war – a crippled, disheartening child indeed, but we've learned to live with it by now. I knew that you would go anyway, you'd leave me, this house, your room where all of your children's toys and books remain side by side with your evening dresses and make-up. That thought comforts me. Besides, it's good for you to go away to live on your own and to escape my overmothering you, the typical fault of a single parent. *Living on her own will make her stronger, she will see the world, it is good for a young person to live abroad and Vienna is only six hours away*: I keep repeating this to myself like some kind of prayer. Except that I know that you didn't intend to leave so soon and so abruptly, not only me and your room, but your university and, more important, your friends here. You left behind so many things unfinished. You left because of the war.

It happened right after the 'Slovenian war' or the attack of what was called the Yugoslav Federal Army on Slovenia on the night of 26 June 1991. It turned out to be only a prelude to the nightmare of Serbian aggression against Croatia and it seems certain that Bosnia will be next. As you know I was in London at that time, glued to a TV screen and a telephone. We both cried. 'What do I do, mama?' you said on that first day of the war but I didn't know what to advise you. What does one say to one's child when the war begins? I didn't want you to panic after the army's attack on Slovenia, even if it is only a hundred miles from Zagreb. One part of me wanted to believe that it was not a real war (whatever that means) because a real war could not happen, it is too stupid, too absurd – an army attacking its own people, it might happen in some South American dictatorship, not in Europe. But there was another part of me that knew this is it and there was no way back. The signs were clear – people already killed in Plitvice and Borovo selo, and the smell of blood that evaporated from the newspaper pages filling the summer air with heaviness, with premonition.

One afternoon, Tuesday 2 July – I remember with the clarity our memory reserves only for traumatic events – we were talking on the telephone and in the middle of our conversation you started screaming, 'Mama, they are shooting next door!' I could hear the shots in a garden next to ours; I could visualize the garden and its high wall covered with roses and bunches of grapes hanging on the vine, the way the sun shone through its leaves at that particular moment of the late afternoon. And I could see you standing there, by the window overlooking it, lost and pale, trembling. You dropped the receiver and then I heard your voice, half cry and half whimper, as if you were no longer a human being but a wounded dog. I can hear it now, every sound that entered the receiver on that day, the distant sound of radio news in the background, the tram that passed by the house and the silence, that sudden silence that followed it. Then your boyfriend Andrej's frightened yet soft voice trying to calm you down. Hush, it's nothing, it's nothing he said, but it was too late because that was the moment when the war began for both of us, and we realized it.

I still think about the sound that you uttered that afternoon. I couldn't recognize it as my child's voice. Because it wasn't a voice, not even a scream of utter fear. It was the sound of someone falling apart, of disintegration. I didn't recognize you because I was losing you. I sat at the end of a telephone line, my whole body weak, lifeless, collapsed. I don't think I've ever experienced such helplessness. Suddenly, an old image came back to me – of the two of us travelling on a train. You were two years old and had fallen asleep in my arms. I looked at your face, your eyelids almost transparent, half-open mouth and forehead with tiny little drops of sweat. You looked so small and vulnerable as if anything in this world could hurt you. I felt such an urge to protect you, like a sharp pain deep in the chest. The very same pain I felt sitting there and waiting to hear your voice again – only now I wasn't there to protect you. If only I was there, I thought, forgetting for a moment that you were grown up, you had to protect yourself and I could only help. When Andrej came to the phone, he said it was probably a drunken soldier, nothing more. I should not worry, he said. But *worry* was not the right word. I was calm. At that moment I knew that if you didn't get out of there I'd lose you. Not from a bullet or shelling, but your mind would crack and you would enter a void where no one could reach you any longer. I know you well, I know how much you can take and I can recognize the signs when you reach the edge. The day after, your voice still broken, different, you told me that almost all of your hair had turned grey. Ever since that day, I thank God that you are not a man, that I am the mother of a woman. To have a son in wartime is the worst curse that can befall a mother, no matter what anyone says.

You could not imagine how lonely I get sitting in your room, a kind of clutching feeling in my breast, a choking knot in my throat. Don't worry, I don't cry, I know you wouldn't like it. I just think of what this war is doing to us, breaking our lives in two, into *before* and *after*. I know that you are all right, as much as you could be living in a foreign country. The most important thing is that you are safe, that you are holding up. Living in a country at war, I try to convince myself that what happened to the two of us is nothing, we are just separated, that's all, we'd have had to face that anyway. It couldn't be compared to what other people have had to go through, loss of lives, of homes, of everything. But in suffering there are no comparisons, I cannot suffer less because someone else is suffering more, any more than I can take someone else's burden of pain. I have my own, as little as it may seem from outside. Our emotions are not based on the objective truth anyway so why should I bother with justifying my feelings? Nonetheless, I do feel guilty in another way.

There are two photos of you that I like best and, as you can imagine, I put them on the wall (yes, I know, you hate it but you have to understand that I need this): one as a girl of three dressed in jeans, with curly hair and traces of chocolate around her mouth. The other one is of a sophisticated young lady holding a cigarette (much as I disapprove of it!) taken when you were seventeen. Is it that cigarette, or rather, the way you hold it, the way you inhale and puff away the smoke, that broad gesture that reminds me of your father. I wonder what he thinks about what is going on here, sitting in Toronto. Have you heard from him recently? We married when I was eighteen and he was nineteen. I was aware that he was from a Serbian family while I was from a Croatian one, but it didn't mean anything to me, one way or the other. World War II was long over when the two of us were born and throughout my life it seemed to me that everyone was trying to escape its shadow, to forget and just live their lives. Your father and I never even discussed the different nationality of our families. Not because it was forbidden, but because it was unimportant to the majority of our generation. It wasn't an issue. Maybe it was a consequence of the repression of the communist regime, of the brainwashing of our education system, the plan to create an artificial 'Yugoslav' nation – the fact is that in the 1980 census 1.5 million declared themselves Yugoslav, people of a nonexistent nation, and interestingly enough, they were all born after the War and approximately thirty years old. Or maybe it was just the natural course of things, I don't know. I just know that we were not interested in the past, in who killed whom and why, but in our own lives. The tragedy and the paradox of this situation now is that you will have to decide, to take his or my side, to become Croat or Serb, to take on and suffer his and my 'guilt' of marrying the 'wrong' nationality. In the war there is no middle position. All of a sudden, you as Croat or Serb become responsible for what all other Croats or Serbs are doing. You are reduced to a single nationality – almost sentenced to it, since nationality in the war brings a danger of getting killed just because of it. I am not talking about who is wrong or who is right in this war, the facts are known by now. I am telling you about the situation when you are forced to choose, to identify with something that has been unknown to you, a total abstraction. But you know it all. 'I am from Zagreb,' you said and perhaps it is the only right answer, to be a Citizen. But not now. Not here.

This war happened *nel mezzo del cammin di nostra vita* so if anything, I should be old enough to try to understand where it comes from and how it started. In fact I could see it coming closer and closer with each passing year, then month, then day. One could detect the gradual return to the past long before 1989 with Milošević's invocation of Serbian nationalist feelings and hatred, first towards Albanians from Kosovo, then towards non-Serbians throughout the whole country – remember how far from us it all looked, how ready we were to deny the coming danger? There were other signs – the tallying up of war victims, justification of war criminals, the resuscitating of old national myths, the revival of religion on both the Catholic and

Orthodox sides. But one could still attempt to see it as a reinterpretation of history, a necessary purge of post-war myths about the communist revolution if only it hadn't been aimed at an entirely different purpose: at national homogeniza-tion and the growing antagonism between the nations. Long before the real war, we had a media war, Serbian and Croatian journalists attacking the political leaders from the opposite republic as well as each other as if in some kind of dress rehearsal. So I could see a spiral of hatred descending upon us, but until the first bloodshed it seemed to operate on the level of a power struggle that had nothing to do with the common people. When the first houses were burned down on Croatian territory, when neighbours of a different nationality in the mixed villages started to kill each other, then it became our war too, of your generation and mine. Not out of ideology, but for the simple reason that it changed our whole life. Yours more than mine, because men from my generation are almost too old – with their grey hair and pot bellies, they'd look pretty silly in those camouflage uniforms. How many of your friends will survive? But what did *you* and your generation born in 1968 know of that past, of the hatred that is haunting us now?

After all, it was your grandfathers who fought in World War II. They had fought as Tito's Partisans, Ustashas or Chetniks. Afterwards, hoping for a brighter future they rebuilt the devastated country according to bolshevik principles, ruled by the Communist Party as the vanguard of the people. All of them lived long enough to see the party become corrupt and repressive, but only some of them lived to see the communist regime begin to fall apart in 1989. Yet, none of them believed that history could repeat itself. It was my generation that grew up in times of scarcity when milk and butter, meat and clothes were rationed (you know what my spine looks like because I still suffer from the consequences of rickets). Sometimes we tasted powdered milk from UNRRA packages – it was so sweet that we licked it from our palms like some special kind of sweet. Or we'd eat yellow Cheddar cheese from the cans, or margarine, or 'Truman's eggs' as we called powdered eggs. People moved to the cities to help build up heavy industry; we all went to schools, education was a big thing then. Married, we tried different combinations to escape living in crowded communal apartments shared by two or three families. We enrolled in the Communist Party as our fathers did, but only because it was so much easier to get jobs and promotion if you did.

In the meantime your generation of the late sixties and early seventies grew up fast. You would listen to your grandaddy's war stories after family lunch on Sundays with an obvious air of boredom. You couldn't care less about it; everything before you were born belonged to the same category of ancient history – World War II, World War I, the Napoleonic Wars, the wars between Athens and Sparta. Sometimes you watched the old movies with Partisans and Germans and Chetniks and Ustashas, but with ironic detachment and the sophistication of someone who knows everything there is to know about Spielberg, Jarmush and so on. You watched us buying better cars to replace the Fiat 750, a colour television, a weekend house on the Adriatic coast. We went together to Trieste or Graz to buy Nike sneakers, Levi's, Benetton pullovers and walkmans for you. And computers – for you too, because we were technologically illiterate. You learned languages – English, of course, was the most important – and started to travel abroad on your own and your values became more and more removed from ours: career, money, but no politics, please. Now you are back in those old movies: you have to declare your nationality despite being barely aware of the past. Maybe at the beginning it looked like a Rambo movie: Ray Bans, Uzis, bandanas tied around your heads. But too many of you have died by now for the rest to believe it is just a game. You no longer watch *Apocalypse Now*, you live it. At least you are defending your own country and I cannot but keep wondering, as I'm sure you do too, what do boys on the other side believe they are doing? For me, every death is senseless because the war itself is senseless – but if there are degrees of senselessness, their death must be the more senseless.

You were already gone when I came across an article in a local newspaper. Entitled 'Will You Come to my Funeral?' it was about the younger generation and how they feel about the war. I remember an answer by Pero M., a student from Zagreb.

Perhaps I don't understand half of what is going on, but I know that all this is happening because of the fifty or so fools who, instead of having their sick heads seen to, are getting big money and flying around in helicopters. I'm seventeen and I want a real life, I want to go to the cinema, to the beach . . . to travel freely, to work. I want to telephone my friend in Serbia and ask how he is, but I can't because all the telephone lines are cut off. I might be young and pathetic-sounding, but I don't want to get drunk like my older brother who is totally hysterical or to swallow tranquillizers like my sister. It doesn't lead anywhere. I would like to create something, but now I can't.

And then he said to the reporter interviewing him something that struck me:

Lucky you, you are a woman, you'll only have to help the wounded. I will have to fight. Will you come to my funeral?

This is what he said in the early autumn of 1991. I could almost picture him, the street-wise kid from a Zagreb suburb, articulate, smart, probably with an earring and a T-shirt with some funny nonsense on it, hanging out in a bar with a single Coke the entire evening, talking about this or that rock-group. The boy bright enough to understand that he might die and that there is nothing that he could do about it. But we – me, you, that woman reporter – we are women and women don't get drafted. They get killed, but they are not expected to fight. After all someone has to bury the dead, to mourn and to carry on life and it puts us in a different position in the war. At bottom, war is a man's game. Perhaps it is much easier to kill if you don't give birth. But I am reluctant to say what should follow from this: that women don't participate, or conduct or decide about wars, because they do. Not as women, but as citizens. As citizens they contribute, support, hail, exercise orders, help and work for war – or they protest, boycott, withdraw support, lobby and work against it. This is where our responsibility lies and we cannot be excused.

I am also not excused for what is going on in my country now. Earlier in this letter I mentioned that I felt guilty. Well, my guilt or responsibility, depending on how you define it, is in believing. It is in the political naivety of my generation (even if '68 taught us how to think politically). We grew up in an already hypocritical atmosphere, not believing in the communist ideology but with the regime still there to be reckoned with. As we couldn't see the end of it we conformed, believing that it was possible to change it into what we insisted on calling socialism 'with a human face'. Lucky Hungarians, for they suffered in 1956, lucky Czechs and Slovaks, who suffered in 1968. What happened to us, then? Under only mild repression and with a good standard of living we in Yugoslavia didn't really suffer.

Recently an American friend asked me how it happened that the most liberal and best-off communist country was the one that now had the war. There are analyses, no doubt, that could give more competent answers to this question. But for me, going back and remembering it all, the answer is so simple that I'm almost ashamed of it: we traded our freedom for Italian shoes. People in the West always tend to forget one key thing about Yugoslavia, that we had something that made us different from the citizens of the Eastern bloc: we had a passport, the possibility to travel. And we had enough surplus money with no opportunity to invest in the economy (which was why everyone who could invested in building weekend houses in the mid-sixties) and no outlet but to exchange it on the black market for hard currency and then go shopping. Yes, shopping to the nearest cities in Austria or Italy. We bought everything – clothes, shoes, cosmetics, sweets, coffee, even fruit and toilet paper. I remember times when my mother who lives in a city only a short drive from Trieste would go there every week to get in stores that she couldn't get here. Millions and millions of people crossed the border every year just to savour the West and to buy something, perhaps as a mere gesture. But this freedom, a feeling that you are free to go if you want to, was very important to us. It seems to me now to have been a kind of a contract with the regime: we realize you are here forever, we don't like you at all but we'll compromise if you let us be, if you don't press too hard.

We were different then, so we are different now: it is we who have the war. We didn't build a political underground of people with liberal, democratic values ready to take over the government; not because it was impossible, but on the contrary, because the repression was not hard enough to produce the need for it. If there is any excuse it is in the fact that we were deprived of the sense of future. This was the worst thing that communism did to people. What is our future now? Your future? No one asks that question and I don't like it. I am afraid this war will last and while there is a war going on even in one part of the country, there is no future. And because I am a typically selfish mother, I don't want you to be deprived of the future too. Once was enough.

Forgive me for this long, confused and maybe pathetic letter, but I had to write it. Stay well, all my love is with you.

Your Mother

18

HIGH-HEELED SHOES

'Have you seen this before?' Dražena asked me, holding a yellow piece of paper in her hand, the certificate that she was a refugee from Bosnia and Herzegovina.

'It took me two weeks to get it. Not because of the red tape – the procedure at the Office for Refugees is very simple even if it takes you half a day waiting in what seems to be an endless queue. But I wasn't able to pull myself together and go and collect it because I couldn't accept that I am a refugee, that this time it is happening to me and not to someone else. You see, even now I hesitate to show this certificate to a bus driver when I go into town. In fact, I befriended him just to avoid that, to avoid having to admit that this is my status in the world.'

Dražena is a journalist from Sarajevo who came to Zagreb in mid-April, on the last day when it was possible to leave the city by normal means of transport before the Serbian army surrounded it, the night before they destroyed the bridge over the River Sava to the Croatian side. 'I didn't mean to leave the city, I had this crazy idea that nothing could happen to me. To the others, yes, but not to me. But then something happened to make me change my mind,' she continued.

'I'd just picked up my daughter Ivana from her kindergarten and as I walked across the street near my house, on the opposite side I noticed this woman. She was ordinary looking, blonde, middle-aged and overweight. She was carrying two plastic bags with some food. It was a late afternoon and I imagined she was heading home from her job in the city. When she was about to cross the street a grenade hit her directly from somewhere above. First she was lifted in the air – for a moment it looked as if she was flying – then she landed at my feet. She lay there motionless with blood coming from what seemed to me like a thousand little holes all over her body. I looked at my daughter. She stood there, with her eyes wide open with horror. She didn't look at me, she didn't move or say anything and when I took her in my arms, she was rigid, as if frozen. The next day we left.'

For more than a month Dražena has been staying with mutual friends of ours. In their small two-bedroom apartment they've given her and Ivana their child's room. But she will have to leave soon – perhaps to go to another friend's apartment. They told me that when Dražena came she expected to go back to Sarajevo within a couple of days, after leaving Ivana with her grandfather on the island of Pag. But two or three days into her stay in Zagreb she heard in a radio broadcast that the building where she lived had been heavily hit by a bomb. For the whole of the week following she just cried and took tranquillizers and nothing could get her out of this terrible state of despair.

I remembered her apartment: it was on the sixth floor of a skyscraper where she lived with her father (her mother died of cancer several years ago) because she couldn't afford to live on her own. When I visited her in the spring of 1991 she took me to Baščaršija, the oldest part of the city where they make the best čevapčići. 'Where in the world could you get such fresh-made čevapčići in the middle of the night?' she laughed. Now Baščaršija was almost entirely destroyed, Sarajevo burned down and Dražena is sitting out in my garden. Behind the wall Zagreb is buzzing, the air is sweet with the smell of a nearby linden tree and an orange climbing rose bush has just begun blooming. It is hard to grasp her words as facts, I think as I look at her: the fact that she has lost her apartment, her job and God knows how many friends. She is telling me how she went to Pag where her father has a summer house to leave Ivana. She is wearing jeans and sneakers, her black curly hair tied in a pony-tail. With her dark tan and black eyes she looks like a mulatto beauty. Looking at her I am trying to detect a trace of recent change on her face and it strikes me as odd that I am unable to see any, as if it were only once I could see pain painted all over her face that I could actually believe her story.

On Pag there is no electricity and the water supply is restricted. Her father doesn't get a pension. Living in a house that he built years ago to benefit from tourism, without any chance now of renting it for a third season in a row, he depends entirely on her ability to make money as a reporter. Because they literally live on fish he catches during the day, she went to Caritas, the Catholic humanitarian organization, for help. They gave her some pasta, flour, rice, sugar and a bar of soap.

'But I foolishly didn't bring anything in which to carry things, so I just took all the supplies in my hands and, of course, I dropped them. Right there, in the middle of the room I dropped all the food – pasta, rice, flour, all mixed up. Other women waiting in line started to scream at me, but I was totally unprepared, no one warned me I should bring a shopping bag or a box or something. And you know what, instead of crying, I burst into laughter.'

She is laughing again, but her words are not registering. I am still looking for something in her face, some traces of war. Finally I realize: she is wearing make-up. This is what is confusing about her, making her situation even more surreal, I think. She has the same face as when I saw her last time but it's as if her make-up is bridging the time, the war, her tragedy itself. This is what fails to fit into the picture of a refugee. However I say nothing.

A few days later she came back, this time to pick up some clothes that I'd prepared for her because she'd left Sarajevo with only one suitcase stuffed with Ivana's clothes. This time my daughter was about too, so she took her to her room to give her a few things. When she came out Dražena was wearing a pair of black patent high-heeled shoes, the kind you'd wear to a party. In fact, she looked exactly as if she were going to leave for a party at any moment. 'Why did you give her those shoes?' I asked Rujana, surprise rising from my voice like hot steam. She looked at me in bewilderment. 'Mother, how could you be so insensitive? What do you mean, how could you say such a thing about your friend?' she said. 'What is so terrible, what did I do?' I replied, trying to defend myself, already sensing that there was more to it than I realized. 'I just thought that because she'll be moving a lot from one apartment to another she would need practical things, not fancy stuff like that,' I said, in a matter-of fact tone of voice. 'Oh, but you are wrong,' she jumped. 'She needs precisely that fancy stuff, as you call it. Because even if she has lost everything, she needs to feel like a normal person, even more so now. Why do you expect her to wear sneakers all the time?'

140

Indeed, why did I think that a pair of high-heeled shoes were no longer appropriate for Dražena, why did I react in that way, I asked myself while my daughter left the kitchen in a fury. Perhaps because to me Dražena doesn't fit into the refugee category at all. The truth is that every time the word refugee is pronounced, in my mind it recalls pictures of women covered with black scarves and poorly dressed, their faces wrinkled, their ankles swollen, dirt under their nails. One can see them wandering through the city in groups with that particular look of lost persons. Some of them beg in restaurants or at street corners or just sit in the main square. Who are these people, I asked myself, realizing at the same time what a strange question it was, a question poised between the cliché established for us by the media and the fact that they are no different from us, only less lucky. *These are people who escaped slaughter by the Serbians*, I could hear my tiny inner voice answering. But I could also hear the other voice, the voice of suspicion, of fear, even anger: *They are just sitting smoking, doing nothing. Waiting. Waiting for what? For us to feed them. They could work, there are plenty of jobs around, houses to be repaired or working the land.* But no, it's easy to say that our city wasn't shelled and our homes burned down, as if the war were only that, as if we didn't have enough suffering of our own. Just the other day in a tram I heard a woman saying, 'This city stinks of refugees.' She said it in a loud voice, while two people, obviously refugees, were standing right beside her. The papers report that in hotels down on the Adriatic coast refugees have torn apart rooms, furniture, wallpaper, taps, lamps, everything, shouting: 'If we don't have anything, you won't either!'

Since Dražena fails to fit this picture I have become aware that something deeper is happening to me, that I am witnessing a more serious process: the creation of a prejudice within me towards these people, something that should be called 'a yellow certificate syndrome'. What I am starting to do is to reduce a real, physical individual to an abstract 'they' – that is, to a common denominator of refugees, owners of the yellow certificate. From there to second-class citizen – or rather, non-citizen – who owns nothing and has no rights, is only a thin blue line. I can also see how easy it is to slip into this prejudice as into a familiar pair of warm slippers, ready and waiting for me at home. And even if I don't like to recognize it in myself, I obviously do believe that there is a line dividing us, a real difference – never mind if it is not me who is defining that line, setting the rules, excluding them. Or is it? Once excluded, they become aliens. Not-me. Not-us. You still feel responsible, but in a different way, as towards beggars. You can pity, but you don't have to give. With this exclusion the feeling of human solidarity turns into an issue of my personal ethics. That is, once people are reduced to the category of the 'other' – or 'otherness' – you are no longer obliged to do something for their sake, but for yourself only, for the benefit of your own soul.

Perhaps what I am also witnessing is a mechanism of self-defence as if there were a limit to how much brutality, pain or suffering one is able to take on board and feel responsible for. Over and above this, we are often confronted with more or less abstract entities, numbers, groups, categories of people, facts – but not names, not faces. To deal with pain on such a scale is in a way much easier than to deal with individuals. With a person you know you have to do something, act, give food, shelter, money, take care. On the other hand, one person could certainly not be expected to take care of a whole mass of people. For them, there has to be someone else: the state, a church, the Red Cross, Caritas, an institution. The moment one delegates personal responsibility to the institution, the war becomes more normal, orderly, and therefore more bearable. The person not only relieves himself or herself of responsibility, but also of a feeling of guilt too: the problem is still there, but it is no longer mine. Yes, of course I'll pay the extra war-tax, I'll gladly give away clothing or food to Caritas or any responsible organization, instead of to the suspicious-looking individuals ringing the doorbell claiming that they are refugees. Because what if they are not real refugees – your help might get into the 'wrong' hands and you'll never earn that place in heaven that you'd promised yourself at the outset. The moment I thought Dražena ought not wear make-up or patent high-heeled shoes was the very moment when I myself pushed her into the group 'refugee', because it was easier for me. But the fact that she didn't fit the cliché, that she disappointed me by trying to keep her face together with her make-up and her life together with a pair of shoes, made me aware of my own collaboration with this war.

Now I think I understand what I couldn't understand before: how it happened that people who lived near German concentration camps didn't do anything, didn't help. In Claude Lanzmann's long documentary on the Holocaust, *Shoah*, there is a scene of dialogue with one of the survivors from Chelmno, the place in Poland where Jews were first exterminated by gas, 400,000 of them.

'It was always this peaceful here. Always. Even when they were burning 2000 people – Jews – every day, it was just as peaceful. No one protested. Everyone went about his work. It was silent. Peaceful. Just as it is now,' he said.

And the survivor from Treblinka said: 'We were in the wagon; the wagon was rolling eastwards. A funny thing happened, maybe it's not nice to say it. Most of the people, not just the majority, but ninety-nine per cent of the Polish people when they saw the train going through . . . they were laughing, they were joyful because the Jewish people were being taken away.'

The third voice I remember is of a woman who lived through the war in hiding: 'I remember the day when they made Berlin *Judenrein*. People hurried along the streets; no one wanted to be in the streets; you could see the streets were absolutely empty. They didn't want to look, you know. They hastened to buy what they had to buy – they had to buy something for the Sunday, you see. So they went shopping, then hurried back to their houses. And I remember this day very vividly because we saw police cars rushing through the streets of Berlin taking people out of the houses.'

But maybe the best explanation as to why people didn't stop the massacre is given by a Polish villager from present-day Treblinka who, in answer to the question whether they were afraid for the Jews, answered that if he cut his finger it hurt him, not the other person. Yes, they knew about the Jews, the convoys, the fact that they were taken into the camp and vanished. Poles worked their land right next to the barbed wire and heard awful screams. 'At first it was unbearable. Then you got used to it,' said yet another villager, a Pole. They were Jews, others, not-us. What had a Pole to do with the fact that Germans were killing Jews?

So we all get used to it. I understand now that nothing but this 'otherness' killed Jews, and it began with naming them, by reducing them to the other. Then everything became possible, even the worst atrocities like concentration camps or the slaughtering of civilians in Croatia or Bosnia. For Serbians, as for Germans, they are all others, not-us. For me, those others are refugees. For Europe, the 'other' is the lawless 'Balkans' they pretend not to understand. For the USA it's more or less a 'European problem': why should they bother with the screams of thousands of people being bombed or simply dying of hunger, when those screams can hardly be heard? Let Europe do something, aren't they working the land next to the barbed wire?

I don't think our responsibility is the same – and I am not trying to equate the victims with those who murdered them in cold blood – all I'm saying is that it exists, this complicity: that out of opportunism and fear we all are becoming collaborators or accomplices in the perpetuation of war. For by closing our eyes, by continuing our shopping, by working our land, by pretending that nothing is happening, by thinking it is not our problem, we are betraying those 'others' – and I don't know if there is a way out of it. What we fail to realize is that by such divisions we deceive ourselves too, exposing ourselves to the same possibility of becoming the 'others' in a different situation.

The last time I saw Draẑena she told me she was okay. She is staying in a friend's apartment until the autumn and free-lancing for a local newspaper. Afterwards she will manage to find something else. She also told me that she is writing a war diary since that is the only way she can attempt to understand what is happening to her. 'And what I find most difficult to comprehend is the fact that there is a war going on,' she said. 'I still don't understand it. It's not that I expect a miracle to end this nightmare immediately. No, no. I mean, it is just hard for

145

me to grasp that what is going on is the war. Do you know what a war is?' she asked, but I could tell from her look that she didn't really expect an answer.

I don't know what the war is, I meant to tell her, but I can see that it is everywhere. It is in a street flooded with blood after twenty people have died in a bread queue in Sarajevo. But it is also in your not understanding it, in my unconscious cruelty towards you, in the fact that you have that yellow certificate and I don't, in the way it is growing within us and changing our emotions, our relations, our values. We are the war; we carry in us the possibility of the mortal illness that is slowly reducing us to what we never thought possible and I am afraid there is no one else to blame. We all make it possible, we allow it to happen. Our defence is weak, as is our consciousness of it. There are no them and us, there are no grand categories, abstract numbers, black and white truths, simple facts. There is only us – and, yes, we are responsible for each other.

And I also wanted to tell Dražena that she should go out and dance in her high-heeled shoes, if only she could.

ZAGREB
MAY 1992

19

DEATH, LIVE

They say that a little girl was killed while eating a pie. It seemed that it happened like this: it was morning, bright and chilly. You ask yourself how that woman, her mother, made the pie in Sarajevo? What flour did she use? What oil? In any case, still half-asleep, the two-and-a-half-year-old girl had been sitting at the table, eating breakfast. At that moment, she heard the sound of shelling. Maybe she was frightened by it, so she ran to her mother – but maybe not. The sound of shelling is normal around here. A shell went through the roof of their house and landed in the kitchen. The girl fell to the floor. It all happened with lightning speed and she was dead before her parents or her grandfather had time to understand what was happening. By the time her father took her in his hands and looked for help, it was all over.

Then a TV camera arrived on the scene. This happened perhaps only one or two hours after the shelling. We see the small kitchen already without the little girl, the floor is covered with brick and plaster debris, scattered shoes, her little boots. The camera zooms in on the roof, on the hole left by the shell. Sky and cold descend through the gap into the kitchen. The father is sitting with his arms on the table, crying. The camera gets a close-up of his blue eyes and his tears – so that we, the television spectators, can be sure they are real, that he really cried, the little one's father.

He has on a white pullover made of a rough peasant's wool. The camera moves from his eyes to that pullover so that we can see a red stain on it, left where he held his girl when he picked her up from the floor – when it was already too late. The blood is not dry yet, the stain is bright red, it looks fresh. I know that raw, hand-spun wool that his pullover is made of. I can feel it under my fingers. It takes forever to dry; soaked blood stays wet a long time. Looking at the blood is nauseating. Still, the camera returns to it several times. This is unnecessary. But there is no defense from pictures like this – and no one to tell us how useless they are.

Now we are in the hospital. This is the first time we see the mother too. She lies on a kind of stretcher, covering her face with her hands. The father comes in, in his white pullover with the red stain, and embraces her. It is clear that this meeting in a hospital room is their first since the little one's death. On camera – for the first time. The mother lets out something. In other circumstances you might call it a cry, a howl. But now it is only a sound of emptiness; with that sound, the woman tells her husband she has just lost everything.

This is the end, this has to be the end. The camera can't go any further into human suffering. Neither we, the spectators, nor the people we can't see behind the camera – a reporter, a cameraman, a soundman – can stand this any longer. This has to stop – I repeat to myself while the camera goes on. Now we are looking at a white sheet with red spots. Red on white, that's the sign of her death. My God, how very bright her blood is.

I don't want the camera to look under that cover hiding her small body. But someone's hand evades my thoughts and lifts the white sheet. Her face, we see her face. Her small deformed face, no longer human, framed by untidy tufts of her black hair, her half-closed eyes. We see a close-up of death. Then cut, a little coffin in the shallow ground. The report is finished. It has lasted three minutes.

A moment later, we become aware that we have just seen the tragedy of one family, filmed only a couple of hours after they lost their child. The whole tragedy has happened on camera. The only thing we have not witnessed is the moment of death. (A take from outside: the shell hits the roof. Then from inside: the girl falls from her chair, in slow motion, as if she's flying. A piece of pie drops from her hand and rolls on the ground. That's it. The reporter is pleased.) Well, why not? By now we should be able to stand that too. It's all in the name of documenting, which we obviously believe in.

In fact, that's probably the only thing we have not seen so far. We've watched headless corpses being eaten by pigs and dogs; scattered body parts that do not belong to anyone, anything; skeletons and half-rotted skulls. Children without legs, babies killed by sniper fire. A twelve-year-old rape victim talking about it on camera. Day after day, death in Bosnia has been well documented. Sarajevo has been shelled by a million shells. In that city 80,000 kids are trapped, which makes it the biggest children's prison in the world. Five thousand of them were killed or simply died.

Fifty years ago this is how the Jews suffered; now it's the Muslims' turn. We remember it all, and because of that memory we have the idea that everything has to be carefully documented. Shameful history must never be repeated. And yet, here they are, generations who have learned at school about concentration camps and factories of death; generations whose parents swear it could never happen again, at least not in Europe, precisely because of the living memory of the recent past. What, then, has all the documentation changed? And what is being changed now by what seems to be the conscious, precise bookkeeping of death?

The biggest change has happened within ourselves: the audience, spectators. We started to believe this is our role, that it is possible to play the public, as if war is theater. Slowly, and without noticing it, a hardness has crept over us, an inability to see the truth. These are the signs of our own dying. The close-up of the dead girl's face was one scene too much because it was senseless. To watch war from so near and in its most macabre details makes sense only if we do so to change things for the better. But today, nothing changes. Documentation has become a perversion, a pornography of dying.

ZAGREB
JUNE 1993

20

LOVE STORY

I have seen their picture in newspapers. It was not clear, obviously taken from a distance: two bodies lying on the Sarajevo ground, two sports bags next to them. Admira is wearing a dark skirt covering the soft curves of her body. Boško is in jeans — what else? — and they both wear sneakers. But one can tell, even looking at that blurred photo, that Admira is embracing Boško as they are lying there, dead. This is how it happened: On Wednesday afternoon, May 19, around 4 P.M., they walked along the Miljacka River in no-man's-land, visible to both sides, the Serbian and the Bosnian. Their escape from the besieged city onto the Serbian side was prearranged; both sides had agreed to let them pass. They had to walk about 1,000 yards, but just before the Vrbana bridge — some fifty yards before safety — they fell to the ground, hit by a sudden burst of a sniper's fire.

I can almost hear that distinctive, short, yelping sound in the afternoon air. Boško died immediately, Admira lived long enough to crawl to him and embrace him. There they stayed for almost a week, rotting in the sun (unusually strong this May), the odor of their decaying bodies mixing with that of the young grass.

It is not known who killed them, and maybe it is not even important. There are people on both sides who saw them walking, then falling. Some of them say the fire came from the Serbian side, others claim just the opposite. However, for the next five days the two sides fought for possession of the bodies. On the sixth night, Serbian soldiers resolved the dispute by snatching the bodies.

Boško's mother, who had left Sarajevo a year before and now lived in Belgrade, had given permission for her son to be buried in Sarajevo. Admira's parents said they would prefer to have them buried in Sarajevo in order to attend to their grave, but they also said that the place was of no importance as long as the two were buried together. And finally it happened: the Muslim girl and the Serbian boy who had loved each other for nine years were put in the same coffin and buried in the same grave at the Serbian army graveyard south of Sarajevo.

Their attempt to escape from the war that threatened to destroy their love as well as their very existence had failed – so had their naive belief that love could overcome all obstacles. But I wonder: What did being a Serb or a Muslim mean to them before the breakout of this war? And when exactly did they realize that belonging to one nation or the other might determine their future? Looking at a picture taken after their high school graduation in 1985 – both of them handsome, smiling as they hold each other – I can hardly imagine that nationality had any important meaning for these kids, or for any of their peers in ex-Yugoslavia. I am not suggesting that they were not aware of such things. They probably were, as much as anyone else around them. But nationality did not matter much: it could not decide their destiny, or prevent them from falling in love.

They were born in the late 1960s. They watched Spielberg

movies; they listened to Iggy Pop; they read John le Carré; they went to a disco every Saturday night and fantasized about traveling to Paris or London. They had friends in Croatia and Serbia whom they would meet in the summer to go camping somewhere along the Adriatic coast. And then the war broke out, and it was as if someone had opened an old history book: Chetniks against Ustashe, although this time Tito's Partisans were not around. It was the absurd, monstrous war of their grandfathers' stories. And now this war descended on them, crushing a whole generation that had been brought up under the illusion that they belonged to Europe, that they had a better, different future in store.

Boško and Admira decided to save themselves. After all, it was not their war. When Boško's mother asked Admira if this war could separate them, she answered, 'No, only bullets could separate us' – as if she knew. This happened only a year ago. The moment Boško decided to stay behind when his mother left for Serbia, Admira and her parents understood it was only love that kept him in Sarajevo. But I imagine that he also decided to stay because neither he nor Admira believed that a war in Bosnia would be possible at all, not really. How could you divide people living on the same floor of an apartment building just because they are of different nationalities? (This is what people from Sarajevo would tell you as late as last spring.) How can you split up a mixed family?

Of course, the power of politics proved stronger than their belief in tolerance and togetherness. After tens of thousands of civilians – their neighbors, friends and relatives – had been killed for no other reason than being of the 'wrong' nationality, Boško and Admira realized that they had no chance. The rest of the world had given up on Sarajevo. And while one can perhaps stand lack of electricity and water, even bitter cold and no food, one cannot stand a state of hopelessness for too long. So, when Boško and Admira decided to leave, it made it easier for them to go knowing that the city they once knew did not exist any longer. Perhaps Admira's friends thought she was crazy to leave for Serbia, being a Muslim. What would happen to her once she arrived there? But how could Admira explain to them that in the war she was nothing – only part of a nation, doomed to be 'cleansed'? She was confident that Boško and his mother would protect her and that in Belgrade there would be at least a chance for survival.

I can almost see her on that evening of Tuesday, May 18, as she takes out her old Adidas sports bag and begins to pack. 'Don't take too many things with you,' Boško warns, as he leaves the house to make sure everything is ready, 'just imagine we are going to visit my mother for a week.' But this time Admira lacks imagination. If she would go for a week's visit, she would not take a photo of her parents, her high school diary, her diploma. She would not take her favorite winter dress (not now, it is spring), her golden bracelet and an old rubber doll that brings her luck.

And she would not sit down to write a letter.

When she finishes packing, it is late at night. The city is strangely quiet as if everyone is sound asleep, tired from this endless war. Admira takes a piece of lined paper out of her notebook. There is only the dim light of a candle in her room, but her eyes are used to it by now. 'Dear mother and father,' she writes. Then she pauses. What can she tell them? that she has to go because Sarajevo is not safe for Boško any longer, that he could be drafted by the Bosnian army at any moment? that they could be separated or killed because they are of different nationalities? or that it is only a matter of time before they *will* be killed by shells in the middle of one of Sarajevo's streets, for no reason other than that they live there? Mama and Papa know it all, thinks Admira, as she sits alone in her room. There is nothing to tell them, nothing to explain. They only need to be sure that we managed to escape the death sentence.

Admira sits for a while, then decides to write about her cat. 'Please, take care of my cat. He is looking at me and meowing as I am crying and writing this. Sleep with him at least once a month and talk to him all the time.' Then she puts out the candle (candles are precious) and goes to bed, staring into the darkness for a while.

The next day it all happened, and this is how I imagine it: On Wednesday afternoon, after briefly hugging her parents, she leaves the house. She must have been very brave not to have shed tears, not to have looked back. As she approaches the river, she can see Boško waiting. It is easy to recognize his tall figure, his nervous gestures. Suddenly she feels that her palms are wet with sweat, but as she rushes to him, she fears no longer. Everything is going to be all right – she thinks – as long as we are together. Then they leave their shelter and get out into the open. They are on the north bank of the river. They do not run. They think there is no need to because they have been guaranteed safe passage. Holding hands, they walk briskly toward the bridge, and all that they hear is the creaking of sand under their feet and the murmur of the river.

The safety zone is not so far away now, and Boško speeds up a little. Slow down please, I can't run, Admira wants to tell him, thinking about how foolish she was to pack so many things in her bag, so many unnecessary things that make it heavy now, too heavy to run. But just as she is about to utter those words, she feels something warm gushing out of her stomach. As she looks down in surprise, she sees that her hands are full of blood. Then pain takes over and she falls on the ground. She can see Boško already lying there motionless, far from her, as if he had been pushed away by some unknown force. 'How strange, I heard nothing,' she thinks, crawling toward him with the bag in her hand, as if they might still have a chance. But before she sinks into emptiness, she lives long enough to come close to him, to raise her left hand and embrace him.

Boško's mother, Radmila, is the only one from the two families to attend the funeral on May 27 on the barren hilltop south of Sarajevo. Admira's parents don't dare come, although the Serbian forces have guaranteed them safe passage. They can hardly trust guarantees from either side. What should we make, then, of the fact that the two families were never at odds? They tried together to help the young couple escape from what finally became their destiny. On the top of a plain wooden coffin Radmila drapes a pullover she has knitted for Admira. Then she throws a handful of dust into the open grave: 'My children, you were blown here by the wind of war,' she says. She has no more words, no more tears. I can imagine her there, her feet sinking into a greasy yellow clay. Even if she was not aware of it, her grief had become our grief. Boško and Admira, two young people who represented the future, were driven into the past by a war from which neither generation could save itself.

ZAGREB
OCTOBER 1993

21

FALLING DOWN

I have three photos of Mostar in front of me. One is a postcard, a sepia-colored photo printed on poor, cardboardlike paper. It is dated September 1953, when my father sent it to us on his first visit to Bosnia-Herzegovina. In the center of the photo is the Old Bridge – all postcards of Mostar have that bridge on them, of course – and a part of the old city. 'I think of you as I walk over this beautiful bridge,' he wrote to my mother and me in Rijeka, Croatia. I can imagine him walking there on a warm autumn day. Coming to the middle, to the place where young boys used to jump into the river to prove their courage, he must have leaned over the stone railing and looked into the Neretva below, quick and silent as a snake. He must have stopped there, overwhelmed by the elegance of the stone construction. When his hands touched the bridge, he must have felt its smoothness and warmth, as if he had touched skin instead of stone. It was as if the bridge had a life of its own, a soul given to it by the people who had crossed it in its almost four hundred years of existence. It was erected in 1566 during the Turkish Empire and, the story goes, the stones were stuck together with mortar that had been mixed with the whites of eggs. Serbs and

Turks, Croats and Jews, Greeks and Albanians, Austrians and Hungarians, Catholics, Orthodox, Bogumils and Muslims – all had stopped at the same spot, rested on the same stone. I was four when he wrote that postcard, and I know that he was certain that one day I would see and touch the Mostar bridge, too.

My father was wrong. I did not make it. I foolishly thought the bridge would be there forever. So I never went to Mostar, never walked from one bank of the river to the other. The bridge that saw so many wars, survived so many years, no longer exists. It collapsed in a second on November 9. All I have to remember it by are these three photos: before, during and after. And I wonder what my father, dead for years now, would have said if he had seen this other photo, the last before the bridge was destroyed. Would he recognize it, ragged and pitiful as an old beggar, with a makeshift wooden roof, black automobile tires and sandbags piled in a futile effort to protect it from the occasional shelling that had started with the war?

When the bridge collapsed, it was Tuesday morning. A pleasant, sunny day, much like the one when my father visited Mostar. The town is only about seventy miles from the Adriatic Sea, so winter comes rather late. The bridge had been shelled since Monday afternoon. People who saw it say its collapse did not last long: at 10:30 A.M. the bridge just fell. As I look at the second picture, I try to imagine the sound of the Old Bridge falling down. A bridge like that doesn't just disappear; its collapse must have sounded like a swift, powerful earthquake, the kind that people in Mostar have never heard before. Or maybe it sounded like an old tree splitting in two – a hollow crack followed by a long silence. Whatever the sound, the river swallowed it in a single morsel. A while later, it was as if the bridge had never existed.

The third photo of Mostar is one I cut out of a newspaper and carry around with me. It is in color and, paradoxically, the most beautiful of the three that I have. The sun shines over the rooftops of the old city, painting the stone houses white. The slightly swollen river, a rich, deep green, rubs along its banks like a lazy, satiated animal. Absent from this beauty, however, is the bridge. There's the beginning of its long stone arch, but if that portion were only ten feet shorter, there would be no trace of the structure at all. Only the sheer logic of the place, a feeling that a bridge belongs there, over the river, between two halves of a medieval town, tells us that something is missing. It's been a little more than two weeks, and I'm still surprised when I look at the photo. When I remember what is no longer there, I feel a spasm in my stomach, a knot in my throat. I feel death lurking in its absence.

I've heard that people in Mostar, even adults, cried when they saw that the bridge had fallen. I believe the reports, for I have seen people who are not from Mostar cry as well. An elderly journalist. A lawyer. A singer, who wept for the first time since the war started. Not so long ago the newspapers published photos of a massacre in the Bosnian Muslim village of Stupni Dol. One picture showed a middle-aged woman with a long, dark knife cut along her throat. I don't remember anyone crying over that photo or others like it. And I ask myself: Why do I feel more pain looking at the image of the destroyed bridge than the image of the woman? Perhaps it is because I see my own mortality in the collapse of the bridge, not in the death of the woman. We expect people to die. We count on our own lives to end. The destruction of a monument to civilization is something else. The bridge, in all its beauty and grace, was built to outlive us; it was an attempt to grasp eternity. Because it was the product of both individual creativity and collective experience, it transcended our individual destiny. A dead woman is one of us – but the bridge is all of us, forever.

The war in Bosnia-Herzegovina is well into its second year now. You would think that nothing new could happen, that, after the concentration camps and the mass rapes, the ethnic cleansing and the slow, cold death of Sarajevo, there would be no room left for imagination. But this war seems to have neither rules nor limits. Just when you think nothing could possibly surprise, something happens – even more violent, more painful, more surprising than before.

Finally – who did it? The Muslims are accusing the Croats, the Croats are accusing the Muslims. But does it even matter? For four centuries people needed that bridge and admired its beauty. The question is not who shelled and demolished it. The question is not even why someone did it – destruction is part of human nature. The question is: What kind of people do not need that bridge? The only answer I can come up with is this: people who do not believe in the future – theirs or their children's – do not need such a bridge. For me, this is the chilling measure of the photo of Mostar without its Old Bridge. This is why I would say that those people – whoever they might be – do not belong to this civilization, civilization built on the idea of time, civilization built on the idea of a future. Even if they rebuild the Mostar bridge and reconstruct it meticulously, they are barbarians.

Holding the old postcard in my hand, I regret that I have not been there. My father is dead. The sepia color is washed out;

the existing postcards of Mostar with the Old Bridge in the middle will probably disappear, too. My daughter will only remember a story about a beautiful stone bridge that, once upon a time, existed in a far-away country shattered by a long, long war. And I myself have no memory of my own of the bridge now, when I need it the most.

ZAGREB
DECEMBER 1993

22

A WINTER'S TALE

A mulberry tree in my yard is covered with ice, its tiny twigs forming a fine lace on my window. Snow in Vienna still has its innocent white color. Christmas is in the air.

I am sitting at my table, reading newspapers that I bought at the train station. This morning, I am reading an article in the Bosnian daily *Oslobodjenje* about food rations in Sarajevo: 150 grams of bread daily per person, 6.5 grams of potatoes, 6 grams of rice. And as I read these numbers, I become aware of the slice of bread I am holding in my hand. I look at it, as if I see it for the first time: How much is 150 grams? Could it be just one slice, like the one I am now reluctantly chewing? Or is 150 grams two, or maybe three, slices? And if so, what can one do with that? I am almost tempted to get up and put the piece of bread on a scale, but then I give up. The exercise would be pointless. How could 150 grams ever be enough?

Then I remember that I wanted to cook potatoes for lunch today – only as a side dish, of course. But as I fix my gaze on the text, 6.5 grams of potatoes is no longer abstract – it is absurd. It can't be even a single potato; as I imagine a plate with it in front of me, not a single one. In *7,000 Days in Siberia,* his memoir of life in Stalin's gulag, Karlo Stajner wrote: 'We got 600 grams of bread, tea and nine grams of sugar today.' I put the newspaper down and look at my table. There is butter, milk, jam, one egg and a cup of coffee. I like to drink strong espresso in the morning. This morning, however, my espresso tastes different. I know that I am not in Sarajevo, but today, looking at snow falling and thinking about bread, somehow I am there. Or, at least, I feel that I am not completely present here.

When I was a child, we used to get packages from our relatives in America. They would send us beautifully smelling soaps and cocoa, pink chewing gum, silk stockings, razor blades, delicious chocolates and cans of instant coffee. I used to wonder what life would look like in a country of such richness. But then I did not wish to be an American. Now I wish just that. Or to be a Swede, perhaps an Austrian, a citizen of any country where there is no war, where people decorate their Christmas trees, have a family dinner and give nice little presents to each other. But I am from the bloodstained Balkans. And even if Croatia is not quite 'there' (which is, at least, what we Croats would like to believe), millions of fine threads link me: language, home, relatives, friends, news. The difference between me and any Viennese citizen is that I can't forget all that.

I am also a writer. Not long ago, I wrote about the coming of winter in Bosnia, about a need to do something to stop the carnage. But reading about rations in Sarajevo only makes me aware of my own failure: it is impossible for me to write about the second winter of dying, hunger and cold, for whatever I write is not going to change a thing. Besides, write for whom? For the politicians? For them, the case is more or less closed. For the international news media? For them, everything has already happened. What story could rival all that has taken place: concentration camps, mass rapes, the suffering of children, the bombing of the Mostar bridge? The world has seen it all before, meticulously documented by countless TV cameras and described by millions of words. The world has even seen live transmissions of death, like the one recently on 'Nightline', when two people in Mostar died in front of the TV cameras, one of them a child. What more can one see?

No one is innocent regarding what is going on in this war. Everyone knows – we all do. Very few people can say that their work has made a difference. On the contrary, there is a growing business centered around Sarajevo and Bosnia, and, sadly, the limelight is too often on the participants, not the public. There are lots of books, theatrical productions, documentaries. Bernard Henri-Levy, a French philosopher, made the film *Sarajevo*. Susan Sontag staged Beckett's *Waiting for Godot*. Jenny Holzer printed the cover of *Suddeutsche Zeitung* magazine with blood donated by refugee women. I don't doubt their good intentions. All I say is that if attention and understanding alone could save Sarajevo, then it would have been saved long ago.

As I sit at my table on a quiet, ordinary winter day, I feel helpless for the first time. My words – any words – have no real meaning. I am sick and tired of them. Finally, all we have achieved with words is to establish Sarajevo as a metaphor for tragedy. So what? Are people there going to suffer less of cold because of our good intentions? Will it help them survive, if they get 150 grams of bread? I doubt it, and this doubt, like an acid, is eating me from the inside. I can write about the war as long as I believe in the power of communication and in my own moral right to do it. But today, thinking of bread and potatoes, I feel I do not believe in that power any longer. I somehow have used all my words, given to me as a writer, to make people understand pain, fear and suffering. With the coming winter in Bosnia, I am afraid that my words would just melt away, like this first snow falling over Vienna.

ZAGREB
JANUARY 1994